THETA HEALING® RHYTHM

FOR FINDING YOUR PERFECT WEIGHT

THETA HEALING® RHYTHM
FOR FINDING YOUR PERFECT WEIGHT

VIANNA STIBAL

HAY HOUSE
Australia • Canada • Hong Kong • India
South Africa • United Kingdom • United States

First published and distributed in the United Kingdom by:
Hay House UK Ltd., Astley House, 33 Notting Hill Gate, London W11 3JQ.
Tel.: (44) 20 3675 2450; Fax: (44) 20 3675 2451.
www.hayhouse.co.uk

Published and distributed in the United States of America by:
Hay House, Inc., PO Box 5100, Carlsbad, CA 92018-5100.
Tel.: (1) 760 431 7695 or (800) 654 5126; Fax: (1) 760 431 6948 or (800) 650 5115.
www.hayhouse.com

Published and distributed in Australia by:
Hay House Australia Ltd, 18/36 Ralph St, Alexandria NSW 2015.
Tel.: (61) 2 9669 4299; Fax: (61) 2 9669 4144.
www.hayhouse.com.au

Published and distributed in the Republic of South Africa by:
Hay House SA (Pty), Ltd, PO Box 990, Witkoppen 2068.
Tel./Fax: (27) 11 467 8904. www.hayhouse.co.za

Published and distributed in India by:
Hay House Publishers India, Muskaan Complex, Plot No.3, B-2,
Vasant Kunj, New Delhi – 110 070. Tel.: (91) 11 4176 1620; Fax: (91) 11 4176 1630.
www.hayhouse.co.in

Distributed in Canada by:
Raincoast, 9050 Shaughnessy St, Vancouver, BC V6P 6E5.
Tel.: (1) 604 323 7100; Fax: (1) 604 323 2600

First published in the USA by Rolling Thunder Publishing.

A catalogue record for this book is available from the British Library.

ISBN: 978-1-78180-074-4

CONTENTS

INTRODUCTION

One day, in introspection, I said to myself, 'I have this amazing healing technique. It has brought me back from heart problems. It has brought me back from a tumor. It has helped me endless times with my relationships, my family, my growth. What am I missing when it comes to weight?'

And then I got the divine answer, and it came like this: 'Vianna, anyone who tells you that you can release weight without exercise is trying to sell you something. You have to exercise!'

I took the message literally and started exercising.

Then, after a little while, I got the rest of the message: 'When you can't exercise every day, your brain has to *think* you are still exercising every day.'

So, I am going to share with you how to find your perfect weight by changing your beliefs using your subconscious mind and the Creator of All That Is.

HOW TO USE THIS BOOK

This book is the companion to my books *ThetaHealing®*, *Advanced ThetaHealing®*, and *ThetaHealing® Diseases and Disorders*. In *ThetaHealing*, I explain the step-by-step processes of the reading, the healing, belief work, feeling work, digging, and gene work, and provide an introduction to the planes of existence and additional information for the beginner. *Advanced ThetaHealing* offers an in-depth guide to belief work, feeling work, and digging, and provides insights into the planes of existence and the beliefs that I believe are essential for spiritual evolution. *ThetaHealing Diseases and Disorders* outlines the programs and belief systems I have found to be associated with certain diseases and disorders and the intuitive insights, intuitive remedies, and supplements that I have found to be of value in healing them.

It is necessary to have an understanding of the processes explained in *ThetaHealing* in order to utilize this book fully. I believe they facilitate physical, psychological, and spiritual healing using the Theta brainwave. When we are in a pure Theta state of mind, we are able to connect with the Creator of All That Is through focused prayer. It is the Creator who has given us the fascinating knowledge you are about to receive. It has changed my life and the lives of many others.

If you aren't familiar with the ThetaHealing processes and want to participate in this program, I suggest that you find ThetaHealing practitioners or teachers in your area. Make sure that they are knowledgeable and you feel comfortable with them, then start a series of belief work with them. If you don't see the results you need, you may want to change to a

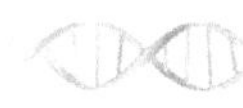

more experienced ThetaHealer or even become one yourself. When belief work is carried out correctly, you will see results.

With study and practice, anyone can find their perfect weight – anyone, that is, who believes in God or the All That Is essence that flows through all things. That is the one absolute requirement with this technique: you must have a central belief in a Creator, a God, the Creator of All That Is. I realize that the Creator has many different names – God, Buddha, Shiva, Goddess, Jesus, Yahweh, and Allah, to name just a few. ThetaHealing has no religious affiliation and will accommodate most belief systems. Its processes are not specific to any age, sex, race, color, creed, or religion. Anyone with a pure belief in God or the All That Is essence can access and use the branches of the ThetaHealing tree.

However, please note that this program may not be for those who have obesity problems caused by specific health problems. People who are medically obese should ask their doctor before starting any exercise or diet plan. An extremely obese person may need an altered plan, and a qualified health practitioner should do a comprehensive study of the person first. I would like to add that I can empathize with the person who is overweight because of health issues, as well as with the person who is overweight because of lack of exercise.

This program is for those who do not have major health problems and who are not lazy but may be too busy to exercise every day. Parts of it can still benefit obese people. It is also my belief that it can benefit those who are underweight because of anorexia nervosa, bulimia, and other psychological conditions.

THE STEPS

There are five steps to the program, and each one is important.

1. Belief Work

The first step is to work on your beliefs, as you may find they hinder you in moving toward your perfect weight. As every layer of 10–20 pounds (4.5–9 kg) is released, for example, you may find that you become nervous about getting thin. You may look in the mirror and get panicky, fearful, and stressed, and just plain feel funny. You may have no idea why you are having these feelings or where they come from. Alternatively, you may remember when you were this weight before and find issues from that time coming up again for you. These runaway feelings have to be stopped and cleared.

2. Supplements

Supplements are suggested for smooth weight release. The main ones are omega 3 fatty acids, apple cider vinegar, and alpha lipoic acid.

Anytime you are fighting with yourself over taking your supplements, you are fighting with some of the beliefs that need to be cleared.

You may also wish to do a parasite cleanse to help release weight.

3. The Heart Song

The heart song is vital to this program. Releasing genetic programs from your ancestors through this exercise will make

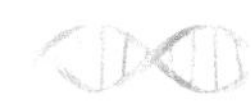

a big difference to how you feel and make you much lighter in general, not just physically.

Interestingly, this is one of the processes that people attempt to avoid. They may be afraid of the sorrow that might be there or just plain find the whole idea overwhelming. However, it is vital to complete this exercise to start releasing weight.

4. Bless and Less

Blessing your food and eating less are also very important. Know that food is not your enemy but your friend.

5. Exercise – without Exercise

We live in a human body that needs to exercise. That is just a fact of life. However, in the final step of this program I will reveal a secret: a way to exercise without having to exercise (much). You will have to exercise a little, but the trick is to get your subconscious to think that you are exercising a lot. What a fun way to release weight – to let your mind do it for you!

When you don't have to fight with your weight, it makes life so much easier. So give this program a chance and see what happens. Many ThetaHealing practitioners have had great results with it, as the e-mails sent to me can attest.

One of the most interesting results has been that those who have started the program *underweight* have felt better in every area of their life after using it. It seems to be a good way of working with people with anorexia or bulimia because they not only feel better when they are exercising, they also feel they are in control of their life again, and control and structure are so important to these special kinds of people.

Please note that even though I am sharing this information with you, I do not accept any responsibility for the changes that can arise from its use. The responsibility is yours, a responsibility you assume when you realize that you have the power to change your life as well as the lives of others.

1

A Beautiful Body

The first thing that you should know is that I think that everyone is beautiful. We are all perfect, each in our own special way. But if you aren't comfortable with your weight, I will show you what to do to become comfortable with yourself and become the person you want to be.

There have been many times in my own life when I haven't been comfortable with my weight. When I was in high school, I was tall and skinny, and people made fun of me. Then I got married and had three children, so I gained weight, but I went back down to an acceptable weight after my last pregnancy. When I was training to be a security guard, I got in pretty good shape. But after the course, I got a security job that required shift work and it was difficult to find the time to run. It was a miracle I was running at all, since for two years prior to my nuclear security training, my leg had been swelling up intermittently. For the next few years it continued to swell up periodically, and this put a damper on my running, too. When it was getting to the point where I couldn't walk on it, I was diagnosed with cancer. From August 1995 to the spring of 1996, I came close to losing my leg and my life. After that I gained weight, just as many people do in times of stress, but I wasn't badly overweight. However, I developed the fear that

I would get cancer again if I were skinny again, so I kept the weight on. I had to work through this fear.

Then, in 1997, the strain from a difficult relationship, a divorce, issues with children, and working 16-hour days began to take its toll on me. I had exhausted myself. I got pneumonia, and that triggered a recurrence of my childhood asthma. The following year, when I started to travel to teach classes, I found that airplanes had lower breathable oxygen content than normal air, and since I didn't have the lung capacity that I should, because of the asthma, I began to take prednisone to help my breathing when I flew. I would taper off the medication afterward, but the side effect was that I gained weight. After six months of this scenario, I had gained 70 pounds (32 kg). I didn't feel good being that heavy, and my body got a little out of alignment, too, because of all the traveling that I was doing. It was horrifying watching my clothing jumping from size to size, ever expanding. I had never been faced with a situation like that before in my life.

Don't get me wrong – I'm not against doctors because of this experience. The doctors I consulted were merely doing the best they could for me, and I know that conventional medicine has its shining moments. However, even though I only used the prednisone for a relatively short length of time, it almost killed me. I had to find an alternative means of healing myself.

It was around this time that I began to notice a difference in how I was treated by other people. When I had been thinner, I would go to a store and the assistants would serve me with courtesy. Now that I was heavier, puffy, and bloated, they treated me with a peculiar disdain. I even had some ask me if I was pregnant!

I didn't like the way I was being treated, or the way I was being perceived. It wasn't even correct! I wasn't pregnant, and I wasn't overeating either. People thought I was eating a lot, but I was actually eating very little.

It was interesting teaching ThetaHealing, too. With some people (mostly women), the fact that I was heavy made it easier, because they felt that I wasn't in some kind of competition with them. Other people, however, would view me with a critical eye. And there would always be the odd person who hadn't worked through their own issues and would come right out with 'Why aren't you skinny?' I found that there were many motives for this kind of 'outspokenness,' ranging from curiosity and competition to just plain nastiness.

Quite frankly, it was easy for me to say, 'Spiritual teachers can be any shape they want to be.' I do view everyone as special in their own way. I think that people the world over have different shapes to their bodies, and they are all beautiful. I look at people from an artist's standpoint: the standpoint of what it would be like to paint them. I have only thought that a person should lose weight when I have been giving them a reading and health issues have come up because of their weight.

During this time I was doing a class in Australia, and at the end of the first day, one of the students came up to me. He was built like a weightlifter and didn't have much excess weight. He said, 'Please, you don't have to answer my question until tomorrow, but I want to know how you can teach a healing class and be so fat.'

This hurt my feelings, and as I left the class that night I told Guy, my husband, in a rush what the man had said. This brought our issues up, and Guy felt annoyed with him, but held back from saying anything to him because the Creator of All That Is told me to not react but to wait.

The next morning the young man came up to me again and said, 'Do you have an answer to my question?'

It is a good thing that God was with me, because otherwise my answer would have been different from the one I gave, which was: 'Why do you want to know?'

He said, 'Because I used to be fat. I had always been fat – all my life. People made fun of me wherever I went and whatever I did and I hated it. I had to do something about it. At first I almost died because I starved myself, and then I started exercising and lost the weight. But you know, even now when I walk into a room full of people, I still feel fat, and no matter what I do, I can't shake the feeling. And yet you can get up in front of a group of people and teach them energy healing without being self-conscious. I want to know what I need to do to be like that.'

Had I reacted to the young man in the way I first thought, I wouldn't have heard the inspirational message he gave me. This gave me food for thought on many levels.

THE EXERCISE LECTURE

When you are overweight, one thing you will always get is the 'exercise lecture.' That random person always just walks up to you and says, 'You need to lose weight – go exercise!'

I'm not a lazy person, and most of you probably aren't either. We are just busy, focused people who lead complex lives and find it difficult to find time to exercise as we should.

So, what can you do when faced with that random person? You can always say, 'OK, when am I going to put exercise into my schedule?'

But then the person will say to you, '*Make* time to put it into your schedule!'

'OK, I will be sure to put exercise in my schedule at three in the morning!'

This conversation is frustrating, as is the obtuse individual who knows nothing about you and the life that you lead.

Air travel is never a good recipe for weight release, for example, and neither is restaurant food. Even 30 minutes of aerobic exercise is difficult at three in the morning at the end of a rather long flight, or after a jam-packed day of teaching, healing, and business meetings. Regardless, you are going to get the 'exercise lecture' from someone!

It was especially frustrating for me, as even at my heaviest I was still stronger than the average person, and most people found it hard to keep up with me, as those who traveled with me soon found out.

For others, especially the obese, it may be difficult to exercise when even breathing is difficult, let alone *moving* without the danger of falling or injury because of the weight.

Let's face it: the exercise lecture really does no good at all…

THE PERCEPTIONS OF SOCIETY

Most people aren't aware of the varied reasons behind weight gain, some of which have little or nothing to do with lack of exercise or eating too much food.

Medical Reasons for Weight Gain

Thyroid problems can cause obesity, as can psychological disorders, and a few cases are caused primarily by genes, endocrine disorders, and insulin resistance. Certain medications cause obesity, such as prednisone, as I discovered. The following is a list of prescribed medications that may cause weight gain in some people:

- Anti-depressants (MAO inhibitors)
- Anti-heartburn medicines: Nexium, Prevacid (may cause weight *loss* with some people!)
- Anti-psychotics: Absenor, Chlorpromizine, Ergenyl, Orfilir, Paxil, Zyprexa
- Anti-seizure medicines: Depakote, Valproate
- Beta blockers (for high blood pressure): Cardura, Inderal
- Breast cancer medicines: Nolvadex, Tamoxifen
- Cortisone and prednisone (used for rheumatism and allergies)
- Estrogen: Follimin, Follinett, Neovletta
- Insulin for Type 2 diabetes: Actrapid, Humulin, Insulatard

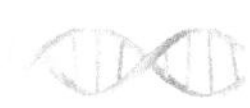

- Lithium: for bipolar disorder
- Migraine medicines: Ergenyl, Sandomigrin, Trypizol
- Mood stabilizers: Cipramil, Elavil, Sertralin, Tofranil, Xeroxat, Zoloft
- Rheumatism medications: Enbrel, Etanercept

This information is not intended to alarm you! Many people don't gain any weight because of their medication. However, practitioners of conventional medicine have freely admitted that some people have experienced weight gain after using a particular medicine. This is no reason to discontinue any medication – that is a choice that should be discussed with your doctor.

There are other things that can cause weight gain that are often overlooked, and these are genetics and a person's belief systems. We will examine these in more detail later.

Overweight vs. Obese

First, a note on these terms, as I have found that there is some confusion over them. Being *obese* means having too much body fat in ratio to muscle tissue. This is different from being *overweight*, which means weighing too much for your body size (mostly as defined by health insurance companies eager to raise premiums). In this case, the weight may be due to muscle, bone, fat, and/or body water.

Both of these terms, however, mean that a person's weight is more than what is considered healthy for their height, age, and so on.

In most people, obesity develops over time when more calories are consumed than are used. The balance between calories in and calories out differs for each person. Factors that might cause obesity include genetic makeup, overeating, eating high-fat foods, and not being physically active. Obesity increases the risk of diabetes, heart disease, stroke, arthritis, and some cancers. This is why it is best for obese people to start with simple forms of exercise such as walking, using a rowing machine, or riding a stationary bicycle at a slow pace.

The unfortunate thing that is likely to happen when someone begins to exercise after long abstinence from it is that the exercise will release toxins that have been stored in the tissues. This can make the person feel terrible until these toxins have gone. This is why it is always best to start any exercise regimen slowly – and why we have come up with a new program for exercising without exercising (*see Chapter 7*).

The Stigma of Being Overweight

As I found, in western society there is a real stigma attached to being overweight or obese. This has become a wide-ranging attitude toward people who are even moderately overweight.

Much of the stigma has come from the modern media using models and bodybuilders to promote everything from clothing to cars. This proliferation of the 'perfect body' has created a false ideal – yet it is to this ideal that many people compare themselves and others. The result of these popular beliefs about weight is that many people think they need to lose weight when they don't need to lose any at all and are absolutely beautiful the way they are.

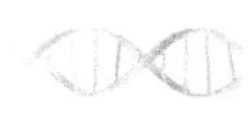

This is also a very modern view. In the past, being fat was seen as a good thing. It is likely that in ancient times we stored fat for the lean periods when food wasn't abundant, or possibly for when we became sick. It was beneficial for the fat reserves to be there when we needed them. Stored fat was a definite plus and could be a life-saver. It may even have been looked upon with some envy.

These associations persisted, and later in history being fat was widely perceived as a symbol of wealth and fertility, as it still is in some parts of the world. I have traveled to countries where people don't believe that you have to be super-skinny, and I have traveled to countries where they do.

In California, the closer you get to Beverly Hills, the blonder, the bigger busted, and the skinnier the women become. They all have to have the 'perfect' body.

I am as unpretentious as they come, and on one particular occasion when I went to teach a class in California, I found my fingernails weren't done to the class's specifications, and neither were my toes. My granddaughter and I always had fun painting my toes, and I wasn't about to forego this pleasure for the class, but the women – all blonde, with perfect makeup – just went crazy because of the appearance of my toes and sent a pedicurist to my room to repair and paint them.

Nevertheless, I found that when I started to do one-on-one healings with some of these women after class, they weren't as self-confident as they appeared to be. I did belief work with some of them and found that while they were outwardly attractive, they still thought that they weren't beautiful enough. Many of them had the benefit of Botox, plastic surgery, hair dye, breast implants, liposuction, manicurists, makeup, and anything else in vogue, yet were unable to accept their own beauty, inside and out. I have found that it is very difficult working with someone whose appearance is essentially perfect to others (and to me) when they believe that they aren't beautiful and are constantly and compulsively striving for even the smallest improvement. To me, outward 'perfection' isn't necessary; it is our character that defines us.

Part of the contemporary focus on being thin came from the clothing models in France. In the past, French designers hired voluptuous, full-breasted, full-bodied women to model their clothing lines. The problem was that everybody focused more on the voluptuous women underneath the clothes than they did on the clothing. The designers then had the brilliant idea of hiring beautiful but emaciated women to model their clothing so that people would pay attention to the clothes and not the models. Unfortunately, the women watching the stick-like models who came strutting down the catwalk all began to think that this was what people wanted to see, and large portions of the western population began to believe that they had to be super-skinny to be beautiful.

There are so many ideas of beauty.... Several years ago I decided that I wanted to become a bodybuilder. I thought that a bodybuilder named Vianna would be a fun thing – and then I found out that there already was a famous bodybuilder named Vianna! I looked at pictures of her. All that muscle! Although I felt that she was beautiful, that was when I decided that a bodybuilder wasn't what I wanted to be after all.

THE ROLE OF GENETICS

Of course our genes play a part in our weight too.... If I go to Japan, I'm going to see very thin people, because they are that way genetically. If I go to the Hawaiian Islands, where the Polynesian people have been swimming in the cold ocean for centuries, I'm going to see people who are strong, but heavy. They have more body fat because of where they live and what their ancestors have done in the past. If I go to countries that are colder, I'm going to see bigger, heavier people. You can see this if you go to more northerly climates: the men are larger and the women are heavier.

Sometimes the size you are because of your genes isn't the size that you would like to be. Some cultures also have different body styles than others. Much of this relates to their genetics and their genetic beliefs.

What is healthy for you from a genetic standpoint may not be what you want to be or how you want to look. But you need to understand that your body shape is special to you. You should aim to be healthy and strong, and full of your own special beauty.

After several years of being overweight, I started to work on a way to return to my optimal weight using exercise and ThetaHealing so that I could be comfortable with myself again. I found that this combination had amazing results when I used it. Let's look at how it can have amazing results for you, too!

2

A Quick Reminder of Belief Work

Belief work is an essential part of ThetaHealing. It is the part that can be easily interpreted and understood from a psychological viewpoint. It is a way to open a portal directly into the subconscious mind to create change within it.

Through observing people in belief work sessions, it seems to me that there is a bubble of protection around the ocean of the subconscious mind – at least in some people. This field of protection is created in a natural process in order that the hard drive of the subconscious can insulate us from pain, or what it perceives might be painful to us, should we attempt to change what ThetaHealing now calls a 'program.'

PROGRAMS

Our brain works like a biological super-computer, assessing information and responding. How we respond to an experience depends on the information that is given to the subconscious and how it is received and interpreted. When a belief has been accepted as real by the subconscious mind, it becomes a 'program.'

Programs may be formed over a lifetime, or they may arise from childhood. When we are children, for example, our experiences with change can teach us that it can be painful, even dangerous. For instance, it can be traumatic to change schools. If other unwanted changes take place, say our parents divorce or a family member or friend dies, a bubble can begin to form around our subconscious as a means to insulate us from the pain. As we grow older, change and growth (as they are perceived by the western mind-set) are also in large part perceived as painful. When we lose or change jobs, lose a lover, or as our bodies age, our perceptions of change can become more and more negative. So, as we grow older, it becomes more and more difficult to make changes that might be painful for us. The bubble stays in place and the layers of protection become thicker and thicker. Belief work is a means to pierce through these layers to the subconscious mind to enable change to be made without creating or re-creating the pain.

Programs can be to our benefit as well as to our detriment, depending on what they are and how we are reacting to them. Many, however, are preventing us from making positive changes, and we aren't even aware of them.

To take another example, many people live most of their lives with the hidden program that they can't succeed. Even if they are very successful for many years, they may suddenly lose everything they own or do something to sabotage themselves because of this hidden program. They don't understand that there are programs deep within them that have been there since childhood, floating in the subconscious mind, just waiting for the opportunity to be reinserted into reality.

Belief work empowers us with the ability to remove these negative programs and replace them with positive ones. It

works through the perception that we can create change through one of the most powerful forces in the universe: the energy of subatomic particles.

DIGGING

One of the ways in which a ThetaHealing practitioner can be more effective in a one-on-one belief work session is to use something that is now called 'digging.' Digging is energy testing for the key belief that is the basis for many other beliefs. The practitioner has the opportunity to play the role of private investigator in the search for the emotional issue that is the root cause of a whole set of other beliefs. As the practitioner energy tests the person, the statements made by the person will give clues to the key belief.

It is helpful here to visualize the belief system as a tower of blocks. The bottom block is the *key belief* that is holding the rest of the beliefs up. You can save hours of time by seeking and clearing the major key beliefs.

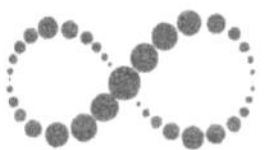

How to Determine the Key Belief

- Begin by asking the person, 'If there is anything you would change in your life, what would it be?' That will lead you to the issue at hand.
- Ask questions pertaining to the issue at hand. Continue to ask questions until you have reached

the deepest core issue. You will know that you are close to the key belief when the person begins to become verbally defensive, wriggles, or cries in a subconscious attempt to hold on to the program. Pull, cancel, resolve, and replace the issue as necessary on whatever belief levels you have found it. The key questions to ask are 'Who?' 'What?' 'Where?' and 'How?'

- Avoid putting your own programs or feelings into the investigation process.
- Be sure you are firmly connected to the perspective of the Creator of the Seventh Plane when you are in the person's 'space,' as in some instances, the issue will loop, hide, or take you in circles with the question/answer scenario. Be patient and persistent with the person to find the deepest program. It may be necessary to ask the Creator what it is. Ask, 'Which key core beliefs are holding this belief system intact?'

Once you are in the process of seeking a key belief, the key belief must be found before the end of the session or the person may experience a healing crisis. Do not leave this person before the belief work is complete, and closely look out for any signs of discomfort. If people feel or act unsettled, or feel any pain or sorrow, then their issues have not yet been taken care of and the belief work should continue.

When clients experience inexplicable physical pain in a session, it is likely that you are reaching deep into subconscious programs. This means that you are triggering different belief

systems that the subconscious is fighting to hold on to. With the clients' permission, ask them to download what it *feels like* to be safe. Continue with the session until the pain has gone and the person is comfortable and has a peaceful demeanor.

In most instances, however, digging must precede the insertions of feelings or the release of programs. The first thing we have to understand is which neuronal connection we need to change, and digging brings us to a realization of exactly what this is.

This process is easy! All you have to do is ask, 'Who?' 'What?' 'Where?' 'Why?' and 'How?' The client's mind will do the digging for you, accessing information like a computer, and will give you an answer to every question. If people seem to get stuck finding an answer, it is only temporary. Change the question from 'Why?' to 'How?'. If there still is no answer, ask, 'If you did know an answer, what would it be?' With a little practice, you will learn how to access the ability of the mind to find the answer.

At any time in the process, the Creator may come to you and give you the bottom belief that you are looking for, so be open to divine intervention.

Always find out how the bottom belief has served people and what they have learned from it. There is generally a positive aspect to most bottom beliefs. For example, 'If I am overweight, my feelings are safe,' or 'If I am overweight, my deepest feelings will stay hidden.' Our mind is always doing its best to protect us from pain.

In my first and second books, I discuss digging for the bottom beliefs in an in-depth and comprehensive way, so consult these

if you require further information. There are also examples of belief work in the following chapter. Remember that digging doesn't mean asking the Creator what to change and nothing more; it involves a discussion with your clients, since the simple act of talking about the topic will free them from part of their issue. It will, in effect, bring the programs into the light of the conscious mind to be released spontaneously.

RELEASING AND REPLACING PROGRAMS

It is always best to find the deepest program of the subject matter you are pulling and replacing before the session has ended. Be sure to include feeling work in your session, since the insertion of feelings in many instances will expedite the process of locating the deepest program.

As soon as you have the key program, ask the Creator whether to release it, replace it, or simply delete some aspect of it. Never replace a program without proper discernment – always ask the Creator. What might at first be perceived as a negative program may actually be beneficial. Programs should not be randomly released.

Once you have modified the synapses as required, ask what the person has learned from having the program that has been replaced and why it was there in the first place. Understanding why people have programs that aren't for their highest and best will help them avoid re-creating the same energy.

Then you have to make sure that you change any associated patterns that might interfere with the new concept. Remember that past lives and genes may also block the insertion of a belief.

The key is in the client–practitioner interaction, but clients must not focus too much on the idea that their brains are being reprogrammed, or the subconscious may attempt to replace a new program with the old one.

Teaching the subconscious new actions is not a novel idea of my own. A variety of processes for changing the subconscious mind are available, such as reading the same thing for 30 days. In ThetaHealing, we believe the changes are almost instantaneous. Beliefs are pulled, sent to the Creator and replaced with new programs and feelings from the Creator.

The results can be wonderful. We believe that by using the belief and feeling work, it is possible to make physical changes to the body, and disease can disappear. I have also seen many lives change as a result of simply downloading feelings from the Creator. For instance, if you insert the feeling and knowing of how to live joyfully, the cells will open the gates for happiness, and the person will act differently from that moment on.

(There are examples of belief-work sessions in the following chapter. For more comprehensive information on belief and feeling work, please refer to *ThetaHealing* and *Advanced ThetaHealing*.)

3

Weight Release Step 1: Belief Work

At first I wanted to release weight through belief work alone. But I found it difficult to achieve results because weight carries so many layers of belief. I discovered that I had to follow up with other steps in order to be successful. However, belief work was the guiding light that I needed and was still the first step.

When I first taught a class on weight release to some of my older students, I saw just how important belief work was. I had just begun to explain the structure of the class when one of my students (who was rather heavyset) said flatly, 'This isn't going to work.'

If you have the belief system that something isn't going to work before you even make the attempt, then belief work is in order. That student obviously had some issues about change and releasing weight. That's understandable, as we get comfortable with the way things are and with being in our own skin. Frankly, changing our outer skin is overwhelming to some of us. But low self-esteem won't cause us to retain weight; it is *fear* that is the real issue.

Weighty Beliefs

As I did readings and healings on people who were overweight, I learned a lot from their mannerisms, from the things that they said, and from observing their overall belief systems. Patterns began to form. I found that many people who were overweight (to the point where it made them unhealthy) had a tendency to be pushy and argumentative due to the pressure that being overweight put on their heart. They had a tendency to be critical of others (particularly with others who were overweight), and a fair number tended to be angry at the whole world. Still others were full of a great sorrow that they couldn't define. We should realize that these feelings are caused by imbalances in the organs, such as the liver and kidneys, not to mention the added factors of self-perception and the snide comments from others.

When it comes to beliefs, people are overweight for many different reasons. Here are the three that I have found the most common:

1. The most prevalent reason why people are overweight is because they feel they should be because everyone else in their family is either overweight or obese.

2. The second most prevalent reason is the belief that if they are overweight, they are safe and protected. Be sure to release the program of 'I am a victim' from them.

3. The third most prevalent reason is that they have what is called the 'overweight gene,' which is an interesting belief system in and of itself. To our ancestors, being heavy was often a sign of wealth, power, and prosperity.

> Energy-test for the belief that being overweight is powerful, safe, and secure.

Overweight and obese people can develop all kinds of belief systems that can be a challenge to overcome. Some think that being overweight is not their fault and play the 'blame game.' Some are overweight to please their spouse on a subconscious level. Many people, both men and women, think that if their spouse is a little overweight, no one will be interested in them, and therefore they won't run away with someone, so their spouse becomes overweight to reassure them. By the way, this thinking doesn't actually deter people from running away with someone. I have seen people who are overweight leave relationships just as often as anyone else. I did find, however, that a good number of women thought that if they were overweight they wouldn't cheat on their spouse.

I myself found that I had a fear of being skinny and being married to Guy. When I first met him, he told me he liked a woman with a little meat on her bones. And boy, did I add the meat. I wasn't afraid that the extra weight would upset my relationship. On the other hand, when I started exercising and dropping the weight, the fear of being thin surfaced. So I wrote down some of the beliefs from my sessions, and some that came up when I started exercising, for others to use.

It is my belief that most people fail to find their perfect weight because of the beliefs that block the process. A good way to tackle this is to make a list of the beliefs, clear them, and then clear any other beliefs that come up during the process.

I was surprised by the beliefs that came up when I started shrinking back down to my normal weight. What happened

was I did really well for two months and then I found I didn't want to continue. That's when the issues starting coming up. Maybe I was dropping the weight too fast – with each pound that was released, old feelings came up, and new ones as well. It was all too much, and that's why I didn't want to continue the process. That was when it was necessary to do belief work on myself.

Given what had happened to me in the past, I expected to have to pull resentments. A lady went home from one of my classes in Australia, pulled all of her resentments (while in the bathtub) and lost two pants sizes. Then I told a class in Utah that the release of resentments could release weight, and another lady lost two pants sizes the same way. I did the same thing and didn't lose anything. My issues weren't resentments after all, but something else, namely generations of sadness and sorrow. In this book there are examples of beliefs that may be blocking you, not only from finding your perfect weight, but also from being beautiful and strong.

With belief work for weight release, something to look out for is to avoid programming people (or yourself) to 'lose' the weight, because if you do, they will look for it and find it again.

It is also important to release overweight people from the *judgments* that others are making about them. These judgments can cause them to become depressed, especially if they are profoundly intuitive. Program them with 'Every bite of food I eat is full of love, and I become content easily.'

Also, check the history and genetic levels for any 'weight means wealth' beliefs and any issues with power or safety. With women in particular, many of the issues you will face

will revolve around guilt, abuse, ancestral programs that sex is shameful, and guilt over dealing with sexual energy. These aspects need to be changed and put back into perspective. If the sexual chakra isn't open, it can be difficult to release weight.

Intuitively stimulating the pituitary is also helpful, as it can release the hormones to counter obesity.

BELIEFS AND GENETICS

From the standpoint of belief work, issues about weight are likely to be deeper than the superficial (core) level that we have learned in this life. They can be as deep as the genetic and history levels. Just as with core beliefs where we can keep inserting the same dysfunctional behavior and reliving the same scenarios with certain kinds of people, the same repetitive issues and situations will keep coming up until they are resolved, and they may be played out on a genetic level as well. This means that the people who are coming into our lives may be mimicking things that our ancestors have already dealt with but not resolved completely.

Some students have finished with the superficial core beliefs and believe that they have no beliefs left to work on, but there may still be genetic beliefs that have never been resolved. Sometimes, sitting down and evaluating your parents' issues with life, as well as what you know about your ancestors' lives, may help you solve issues with weight.

These parental issues may relate to the events that happened in your parents' lives – what they didn't accomplish and/or other issues that have never been solved. If your parents were thin and you are heavy, you are likely to be carrying a number of issues that have been handed down to you from your parents and not from the ancestors before them.

For instance, I don't think that my mother ever forgave herself for things that she did (and didn't do) in the past. She looked for one true love all of her life but didn't find it. It was likely that this was because she had a difficult time with relationships and at some point decided not to take the chance of being hurt anymore. I think that the yearning to find love was passed on to me. So when I fell in love with Guy, it was as if I was fulfilling a desire that my mother had had all her life.

Forgiving yourself for the past can bring about a significant change in yourself and in the way that you affect your children.

What was fascinating to me was watching people who took our ThetaHealing World Relations class begin to drop weight after they worked on their issues that pertained to their ancestors. They were releasing generational prejudices that they didn't understand and didn't know they had.

We have to understand that DNA is much more complex than we give it credit for. It holds memories, feelings, and lessons that must be learned.

Incidentally, when it comes to finding your perfect weight, I'm assuming that thin is mostly what you want to be? I suggest you go for the goal of being strong instead. You are fighting so many genetic programs when it comes to the word 'thin.' Think about it: the starving person is the one who's thin. The one who has no money is usually starving *and* thin. You could work all day pulling these ancient and modern beliefs, or you could just say, 'I am strong.' 'Strong' for most people means

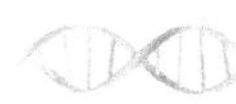

'thin,' but it is the negative connotations to 'thin' that the subconscious mind will latch on to.

LAYERS OF BELIEF

I believe that this world is more of an illusion than we realize. We all project an image to others. And we believe ourselves to be the person we look at in the mirror, but are we really? What I am going to do is to shift that image for you by teaching you to love yourself and also to love your body so that it can become what you want it to be instead of being stuck at a certain weight.

So, the first part of our program is to work on the beliefs that are associated with not being at your perfect weight.

Later in this chapter is a list of beliefs that you can energy-test for that may be blocking you from releasing weight. This list is not all the beliefs that people have about being overweight. People want to be overweight for many reasons – as many reasons as they want to be skinny. They also have dual belief systems. The list of beliefs that I offer here is just a guide to get you started, and since we are all different individuals, they may only be the tip of the proverbial iceberg. Any belief that makes you put on weight may have many other beliefs attached to it. In fact, it is when you begin to release weight that you will uncover the layers, one by one.

How do we end up with so many layers of belief? One of the reasons is that we don't gain weight all at once. Even though it took me only a short time to put on the weight that I gained, it still took months to do it, and there were a lot of feelings along the way! Every time that we gain weight, we lock beliefs in the physical body and create a layer of belief as well as a layer of weight. The weight gain should, in fact, be perceived as gaining layers of belief. And in reverse, when we release the weight, a layer is opened, much as an onion is peeled, and the beliefs and toxins inside are released.

So, when you drop a layer of physical weight, an issue will come up, and so on and so forth until each layer and its subsequent beliefs have been released. The layers are different with everyone and may present themselves when you have lost 2 pounds or 20. You may have lost someone close to you when you were at a certain weight, for example, and this grief may come up when you reach the same weight again. The reason this happens is because every cell in your body has a full memory of everything that you experience, and that includes fat cells, too.

This means that some of our 'weight issues' may not be what we think they are. It is also the reason why we may drop, say, 10 pounds (4.5 kg) and then turn around and gain them all back in short order. If we haven't released the beliefs and feelings that are associated with the physical weight in that layer, we will regain it. This is why belief work is a vital aid in releasing weight. It may involve some psychological questioning, but the time spent on it is likely to be beneficial.

BELIEFS AND DOWNLOADS

The following are some beliefs and downloads pertaining to weight-release layer work. These beliefs may not have anything to do with food or being overweight when the bottom belief is found in a digging process.

Energy-test the client (or yourself) and see if they (or you) have one of these beliefs. Any program that has to do with 'I am overweight' or 'I am fat' should be replaced. 'I am overweight' should be replaced with 'I am slender and strong' or 'I am healthy.'

You will find that beliefs about being overweight are usually carried at least to the genetic level. In some tribes, especially Hawaiian tribes and some Native American ones, the heaviest person was the most powerful person. The hidden beliefs would be:

- 'I am powerful when I am overweight.'
- 'I must gain weight to be intuitive.'
- 'I am heavy.'

Be sure to test for these programs at the history level.

With obesity, always start by making sure that you program people (or yourself) that they are strong, and then start digging for the bottom belief.

Once you have tested for the beliefs in this chapter, you should dig to see how far they go, and find the bottom belief attached to each one.

Relationships

Energy-test for:

- 'If I release weight, I will cheat on my spouse.'
- 'If I am heavy, I will avoid relationships.'

- 'I am overweight to avoid attention from the opposite sex.'
- 'I fear being emotionally hurt.'
- 'I am afraid of love.'
- 'My husband/wife/partner wants me this way.'
- 'My husband/wife/partner wants me to stay heavy.'
- 'I am overweight so that I am noncompetitive.'
- 'I am overweight so that I don't intimidate others.'
- 'I am overweight so that I can be taken seriously.'
- 'I am overweight so that I am loved for my mind and not my body.'
- 'I hate being looked at as a sex object.'

If the answer to any of the following is 'no,' there is belief work to be done:

- 'I am impervious to any anger or jealousy from others.'
- 'I am aware that once I release weight, people's perspectives will change about me.'
- 'As I change, I can earn more respect.'
- 'People respect and look up to me.'
- 'I can accept the respect of others with grace and ease.'
- 'People around me can let me get better.'
- 'I am content with how I treat others.'

- 'I treat others with kindness and respect.'

Food

Energy-test for:

- 'Food is bad.' (If you test 'yes,' there is belief work to be done.)
- 'If I lose weight, I won't belong.'
- 'Food is evil.'
- 'I eat less.' (If 'no,' there is belief work to be done.)

Download:

- 'I enjoy the food that I eat.'
- 'I like fruit.'
- 'I like raw vegetables.'
- 'I enjoy fruit and vegetables.'
- 'I enjoy good protein foods.'
- 'The right kinds of food make me happy.'
- 'I take responsibility for what I eat.'
- 'I enjoy eating less.'
- 'Small portions of food are satisfying.'
- 'I enjoy taking my vitamins.'
- 'I like drinking water.'

Exercise

Energy-test for:

- 'I hate exercise.'
- 'It takes too long to get a result with exercise.'
- 'Exercise is painful.'
- 'There is no time to exercise.'

Download:

- 'I enjoy exercise.'
- 'I exercise every day.'
- 'Exercise is my friend.'

Weight

Energy-test for:

- 'I am too old to release weight.'
- 'If I release weight, I won't belong in my family anymore.'

Download:

- 'I am willing to release excess weight.'

Beauty

Energy-test for:

- 'If I'm beautiful, people will think I'm shallow.'
- 'If I'm handsome, people will think I'm shallow.'

- 'Beautiful, shapely people are stupid.'

Download:

- 'If I'm beautiful, people will still like me.'

Slenderness and Strength

Energy-test for:

- 'If I am slender and strong, I will become jealous of others.'
- 'If I am slender and strong, others will become jealous of me.'

Download:

- 'I know how to live without the fear of change.'
- 'Change is good.'
- 'I can be slender and strong if I choose to.'
- 'If I am slender and strong, people will still love me for who I am.'
- 'I see myself as attractive and slender.'
- 'The mirror is my friend.'

BELIEFS AND FEELINGS DOWNLOADS

Mind, Body, and Soul

- 'I am slender and attractive.'
- 'I am close to God in a healthy, strong body.'

- 'The stronger I become, the closer to God I become.'
- 'God loves me whatever shape I am.'
- 'I love my body.'
- 'My body is energized.'
- 'My body saves energy.'
- 'My body is strong.'
- 'My body gets stronger every day.'
- 'My body understands how to regulate my sugars.'
- 'With each passing day, the systems of my body get stronger.'
- 'I am young.'
- 'I am strong.'
- 'The stronger I am, the kinder I am.'
- 'I can be strong.'
- 'I enjoy exercise daily.'
- 'I feel good about myself.'
- 'I am important.'
- 'I am confident about releasing weight.'
- 'I am patient with myself.'
- 'I am calm and collected.'
- 'I am amazing.'

- 'I am brilliant.'
- 'Everything that I have done in life matters.'
- 'I like who I am.'
- 'I am proud of my life and how I have lived it.'
- 'The Earth can let me get better.'
- 'I am full of energy and strength.'
- 'I use my words wisely.'
- 'I breathe the breath of life.'
- 'When I am tired, I find energy from the breath of life.'

Food

- 'I know when I am full.'
- 'I know how to stop when I eat.'
- 'I know how to eat less.'
- 'I know how to nurture myself without overeating.'
- 'I understand what it feels like to eat less.'
- 'I understand the definition of eating right.'
- 'I know it is possible to eat right.'
- 'I know it is possible to eat less.'
- 'I understand what it feels like to eat right.'
- 'I know how to eat right.'
- 'I know how to live my daily life eating right.'

- 'I know the perspective of the Creator of All That Is on eating right.'
- 'I know how to live my daily life eating healthy food.'
- 'I know when I need to eat.'
- 'I understand what it feels like to eat foods that are good for my body.'
- 'I know how to absorb nutrients from the food that I eat.'
- 'I understand what it feels like to absorb nutrients from food.'
- 'I know how to eat good food, vitamins, and mineral supplements without shocking my body.'
- 'I know when my body needs energy.'
- 'I know how to take care of my body.'
- 'I know how to live my daily life without overeating.'
- 'I know how to cherish and care for my body with dignity.'
- 'I know how to follow through and take vitamins and supplements that are good for me.'
- 'I know how to communicate with my body from the perspective of the Creator.'

Beauty

- 'I understand the definition of beauty through the Creator of All That Is.'
- 'I understand what it feels like to be beautiful.'

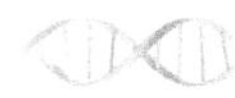

- 'I know how to live my daily life in beauty.'
- 'I know beauty through the Creator of All That Is.'
- 'I know it is possible to be beautiful.'
- 'I know what it feels like to be beautiful.'
- 'I understand the definition of being attractive and thin.'
- 'I understand what it feels like to be attractive.'
- 'I know it is possible to be attractive and thin.'
- 'I feel safe in a relationship.'
- 'I feel safe with others.'

Weight Release

- 'I understand what it feels like to release weight daily.'
- 'I understand what it feels like to exercise.'
- 'I know how to exercise responsibly.'
- 'I understand what it feels like to replace eating with exercise.'
- 'I understand how to feel good about myself.'
- 'I know how to live my daily life without overeating.'
- 'I know how to live my daily life without being discouraged about my weight.'
- 'I understand the definition of weight release.'
- 'I know how to release excess weight.'

- 'I know how to exercise.'
- 'I understand what it feels like to drop weight.'
- 'I know how to drop weight.'
- 'I know how to live my daily life exercising.'
- 'I know it is possible to exercise.'
- 'I understand what it feels like to exercise.'
- 'I know how to live my life without exposing myself to toxic substances.'
- 'I know how to acknowledge my own physical needs.'
- 'I know what it feels like to be energized and accepted.'
- 'I know how to control my moods when I feel tired.'
- 'I know when I am getting tired.'
- 'I understand how to feel good about myself.'
- 'I know how to utilize the life-force in the highest and best way.'

Health

- 'I understand the definition of health through the Creator of All That Is.'
- 'I understand what it feels like to be healthy.'
- 'I know when I am healthy.'
- 'I know how to be healthy.'

 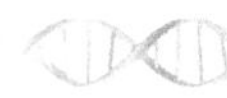

- 'I know it is possible to be healthy.'
- 'I know how to live my daily life in health.'
- 'I know the perspective of health through the Creator of All That Is.'

BELIEF WORK SESSIONS

Some of the fears that may come up when you release weight are fears that you may become what you have hated for many years. Many people who are overweight hate skinny, attractive people and are afraid that if they release weight, they will be hated, too. They think attractive people are shallow, and are afraid that they will become shallow if they become more attractive. They are afraid that their personality will change, that the attitude of those around them will change, and that they will lose what they have learned. They also think that their family will no longer accept them if they lose weight.

The overweight person has to come to the realization that this fear of loss is only a *fear* and isn't a reality. It is true that some people change when their looks change, but this doesn't have to happen. The following belief-work session is a good example of the fears involved in this scenario.

Belief Work: What will happen when weight is released?

This session is with a young overweight woman.

Vianna: 'I want you to envision yourself in the future. I want you to see yourself thinner, to see how you want your life to be, and to see what is going to happen.'

Client: *'I'm happy with my weight as it is – at least I'm not unhappy with my weight. I really am happy the way I am. I'm proud of my accomplishments, and I've done a lot in my life. I'm comfortable with who I am. If I lose weight, I will find somebody, and I will have to be in a relationship, because that is what happens when you lose weight.'*

Vianna: 'Now wait a minute – you said that you wanted to lose weight, and now you are saying you're happy with your weight.'

Client: *'Well, I guess I do need to lose weight, but for my health, not for a man.'*

Vianna: 'OK, let's talk about why you won't lose weight for a man. What do you mean?'

Client: *'Well, if I get thinner, my family will expect me to find a husband, and if I do find a husband, I will have to be different – I will have to become somebody else.'*

Vianna: 'So, let me get this straight: If you get thinner, you will have to find a man. Don't you want to find one now?'

Client: *'No. If I find a man now, he won't want me for who I am.'*

Vianna: 'Wouldn't you like someone to be attracted to you?'

Client: *'Well, I guess so.'*

Vianna: 'All right, let's start all over again. You want to lose weight, correct?'

Client: *'Yes.'*

Vianna: 'What's going to happen if you lose weight?'

Client: *'My mother is going to be jealous, my sister is going to be angry, and I'm going to have to change my life.'*

Vianna: 'Why will you have to change your life?'

Client: *'Because I will be thinner, so I will have to date again.'*

Vianna: 'Are you afraid of dating?'

Client: *'The last few relationships haven't worked out.'*

Vianna: 'What does that mean?'

Client: *'I loved them and they left me, so I just don't want to date anymore.'*

Vianna: 'OK, you don't want to get into a relationship.'

Client: *'Well, I want* someone, *but not really. Everybody thinks that I have to be with someone.'*

Vianna: 'Do you know what it feels like to be loved for who you are?'

Client: *'Well, they said they loved me, but when they found out who I really was, they didn't love me anymore.'*

Vianna: 'Is that what happened?'

Client: *'I think so. But I don't really know.'*

Vianna: 'Would you like to know what it feels like to love someone and let them in to love you?'

Client: *'Yes, I would.'*

Vianna: 'Let me download you what it feels like to be loved and to let someone love you. Now, do I have permission to teach you that you can release weight and be comfortable with yourself? That you can take your time getting into a relationship if you want to?'

Client: *'Yes, that's what I really want. I don't want to feel that I* have *to be with somebody.'*

Vianna: 'OK, so let's download the feeling and knowing of these things. Now, if you did have somebody who really loved you for who you were, what would happen to you?'

Client: *'I don't know. I really don't know who I am.'*

Vianna: 'Would you like to know yourself?'

Client: *'Well, I know who I'm* supposed *to be – my mother tells me who I'm supposed to be, and my sister tells me who I'm supposed to be, and so does my brother.'*

Vianna: 'Would you like to know that *you* can create who you want to be?'

Client: *'Yes, I want to do that.'*

Vianna: 'Would you like to know that you can be slim, beautiful, and strong?'

Client: *'Yes. I want to be strong, but I'm afraid of being slim.'*

Vianna: 'What's going to happen if you're slim?'

Client: *'I don't know – I've never really been slim.'*

Vianna: 'Would you like to know that you are ready to make a change and you can be slim, beautiful, healthy, and strong?'

Client: *Yes, I want to be those things, but I do kind of like the way I look. I don't hate myself and think that I am fat.'*

Vianna: 'Do you think that you need to lose weight?'

Client: *'I think that I need to lose a few pounds.'*

Vianna: 'Well, how much do you want to lose?'

Client: *'It wouldn't be bad if I lost, you know, 60, 70 pounds.'*

Vianna: 'Is that what you want to lose?'

Client: *'Well, I would like to know what it feels like to be really pretty and to be slim. But if I am pretty and slim, I won't be me anymore.'*

Vianna: 'What makes you think that you won't be you?'

Client: *'Because I will change. They all change. When they get pretty, they all change.'*

Vianna: 'Would you like to know that you can look pretty *and* be the person you want to be?'

Client: *'Yes, I do.'*

Vianna: 'Do I have permission to check if you know what it feels like to be pretty, how to be pretty, and that you are allowed to be pretty and still be who you are?'

Client: *'Yes, I would like that.'*

Vianna: 'Would you like to know that you are lovable and desirable?'

Client: *'Yes, I would like that.'*

Vianna: 'Would you like to know that you can be comfortable and become the person that you want to be?'

Client: *'Yes, I would like that.'*

I download her with the feelings and knowing that we discussed, and then I energy test her to see if she is ready to release some weight.

She tests positive for being ready to release weight, so then I have her visualize what it feels like to be slender and strong.

Again she makes the 'My sister and my mother will be angry with me' statement.

This might be true, so I can't program that it won't happen to her. Instead I download her with, 'It's OK to be slender and strong and still be loved.' I also download her with 'I don't have to be heavy to be part of my family.'

Have we done enough belief work for her to start releasing weight? Definitely. Is there more belief work to be done? Of course there is, but this will come after she has released her sadness with the heart song.

This belief-work session also addressed the issue of being loved for who you are. I love the metaphysical women who say, 'I want someone to love me for me.' Well, the prospective mate can love you for who you are now, or they can love you when you are slimmer. And you might love yourself more if you are slimmer and you might not!

To some, weight release is a life-transforming change. To others, it isn't. Much depends on the motivation and the belief systems of the person who wants to release weight.

For instance, I knew a woman who became heavy through multiple childbirths over a period of years. One day she decided that she'd had enough of being overweight and decided to get a 'stomach staple' operation. When she told me that she was going to have the surgery, I was concerned, as I knew the procedure could be dangerous. Often, people who have it done have to take vitamin B shots for the rest of their life to be certain they are absorbing enough nutrients.

Regardless, the woman went ahead with the surgery, and over the period of a year, she lost a great deal of weight and had to get all the extra skin that was left over cut off.

She lost so much weight, in fact, that she was left with small breasts, so she went under the knife again and got breast implants. She got an infection from that operation and was very sick for a while.

After about a year of this odyssey, she was finally healed up and finished with surgeries, but she could no longer eat very much and she couldn't drink soda pop.

When she was done, she had the body of a 20-year-old woman and a face that looked like that of a wrinkled 90-year-old because of the amount of fat that had gone from it. I didn't know her anymore! Her body didn't adjust well to the change either – it was as if someone had stuck a pin in a balloon and let all the air out.

Anyway, as soon as she got skinny and felt different about herself, what do you think she did? She started to become resentful and vicious toward the husband she had been with since college.

'You've been mean to me all these years,' she said, 'and we are rich now, so I will take half the money and leave.' And she did.

So, what was the motivation behind her surgical weight release? Was it to get skinny and leave her husband, or was it a subconscious program that she was acting out without knowing it? We will never know for sure, and she may not either.

Admittedly, most people won't be at the point of wanting these kinds of surgery. And most doctors will only perform these

operations if they believe that the benefits outweigh the risks. That particular woman was an extreme case. The moral of her story is that if you want to release weight, release it at a pace that is healthy for you. When you begin to exercise, you may find that you are releasing 2–3 pounds (around 1 kg) on any given day, but you may only lose 15 pounds (7 kg) a month. This will allow your body and the world around you to adjust to the change. Your subconscious mind can keep up with the changes, too, and you can have a healthy weight release as opposed to an unhealthy one.

What most people need to do is address their beliefs so that their subconscious can shift the way that they perceive themselves – in a comfortable fashion!

Here is another example of how underlying beliefs can affect weight … and relationships.

Belief Work: Jealousy

This session is with a young overweight woman.

Vianna: 'Do you want to lose some weight?'

Client: *'I do. I want to be thin and strong, the way I used to be.'*

Vianna: 'All right, I want you to close your eyes and take a deep breath and visualize what it feels like to be strong, slim, and healthy.'

The client begins to squirm around on her chair.

Client: *'This feels great! I feel good.'*

Vianna: 'OK. How is the world going to treat you when you are slim, strong, and healthy?'

The client gets very uncomfortable.

Client: *'I will have to do it over again.'*

Vianna: 'Do what again?'

Client: *'The jealousy thing. My husband will think that I'm going to run off with someone, and we will start this whole jealousy thing again.'*

Vianna: 'What jealousy thing?'

Client: *'He gets angry when I'm pretty and strong, and he becomes insecure. He thinks that I will leave him, and we have these terrible fights. It's horrible. So I don't think that I want to be slim, just strong and healthy.'*

Vianna: 'All right. I want you to visualize yourself as strong and healthy.'

Client: *'It's wrong for him to do that to me.'*

Vianna: 'Would you like to know that you can be strong without causing this extra jealousy?'

Client: *'Oh, it's impossible! He's always jealous, and if I were strong, it would only make things worse.'*

Vianna: 'Would you like to know how it feels to know that you are loyal; that everything is clear and good and that you can work these things out with him?'

Client: *'It's ridiculous. I* can't *work these things out. He's always like this.'*

Vianna: 'How long has he been like this?'

Client: *'I don't know exactly. He was like it when we first met.'*

Vianna: 'How long have you been together?'

Client: *'We have been together for 15 years.'*

Vianna: 'Does he love you?'

Client: *'Yes, he does. He loves me.'*

Vianna: 'Does he trust you?'

Client: *'He trusts me now that I am heavy.'*

Vianna: 'Ask him if he will trust you if you are slender.'

Client: *'OK, I will.'*

Vianna: 'Would you like me to show you that you can be both slender and loyal?'

Client: 'OK.'

Vianna: 'Out of curiosity, would you cheat on him or leave him if you were lighter?'

Client: *'Maybe.'*

Vianna: 'Do I have permission to show you that you can be loyal and strong if you release weight?'

Client: *'OK.'*

Belief work like this can help during the entire process of finding your perfect weight. Utilizing belief work as you move toward your perfect weight will make the process smoother. It will help you deal with any feelings that come up and the reasons why the weight was gained or lost in the first place.

4

Weight Release Step 2: Suggested Supplements for Smooth Weight Release

When you begin to release weight, I suggest that you use the following supplements to help provide replacement energy for the weight that will soon be gone. I know that many people don't like taking supplements, but the supplements that I am suggesting here will not only give you energy but also help you over the crisis point when you first begin to exercise.

CRISIS? WHAT CRISIS?

When you begin an exercise routine, many things may be stirred up and released into your bloodstream, including waste products. Your body is engineered to pull out waste products on a regular basis, but when more waste products are produced (or put into the body) than can be cleared, these excess toxins are encapsulated by fat cells in order to neutralize them. Waste products from yeast and heavy metals, for example, can be encapsulated in the fatty tissues of the body. So, when you exercise and reach the point where you are burning fat, you are releasing these toxins into your system once again. If this happens too quickly, you begin to feel tired, your muscles ache, and you may have a whole plethora of other symptoms, depending on the toxin that is being released into the body.

What happens when you resolve to exercise every day? Typically, at the end of the first day, you say to yourself, 'Hey, I did it! That wasn't so bad!'

At the end of the second day, you say to yourself, 'OK, I'm a little sore, but it's not too bad.'

At the end of the third day, you say to yourself, 'I didn't want to do it, but I did it! Only now I'm tired, my muscles are sore, I don't feel very good, and I really hurt…'

When the time comes to exercise on the fourth day, you say to yourself, 'I'm tired, I hurt everywhere, and I think that I have to rest tonight! That's enough exercising!'

What is happening in the body is the toxins are being released into the system from the fat cells, overwhelming the liver and making you feel tired. So the body sends the only message that it can to the brain, and that is: 'For goodness' sake, are you crazy? Stop exercising already!'

The whole scenario is a paradox, because the more you exercise, the better your muscles can release the cortisone that the body needs to relieve pain and make you stronger, but because you are exercising, the body is overwhelmed by toxins and you are feeling terrible, so before the muscles can take over and do their thing, you stop exercising.

SUPPLEMENTS

Supplements can help here. One of the reasons for this is psychological: many people prefer to take an active part in their own healing, and if they don't believe a healing can work instantly, they'll often believe a supplement can do the trick. In this respect, some people do really well with supplements.

Some supplements affect the body immediately, and the effects can be seen in 30 minutes to three hours (if you need the supplement, that is). With the skin, however, it may take about three weeks to see a change.

If you are taking supplements and you aren't feeling any better, or aren't seeing a change at all, your body probably isn't breaking them down correctly and/or you've given up on the idea of using them in the first place. In our health-conscious society most people have cupboards full of vitamins and supplements that they have tried or are currently using. This makes some of the supplements I am suggesting a hard sell, at least to some people. I'm also aware that there are people who don't have the discipline to take supplements every day. There are also people who believe that they should get all their nutrition from food and so are reluctant to take supplements at all.

The chief problem with taking supplements, however, is consistency. When I was seeking to release weight, I would keep a bottle of supplements at home and a bottle at work, so if I forgot to take a supplement in the morning at home, I could take it at work.

SUGGESTED SUPPLEMENTS FOR WEIGHT RELEASE

Here are some supplements that might be useful in your weight-release program. They will help with the elimination of the physical toxins that may be released along with the weight.

1. Molybdenum, omega 3s, apple cider vinegar, and ALA are all a must.

2. The second most important batch of supplements is lecithin, Resveratrol, and the amino acids.
3. DHEA, vitamin E, grapefruit extract, cactus juice, and noni are optional.

Beware! If you choose to use additional supplements, note that many of the herbals that benefit those who are obese can be dangerous. They place strain on the organs of the body, because they have a form of caffeine in them. For instance, ephedra (ma hung) stimulates the heart to beat faster and more strongly. Some herbalists combine ephedra with guarana, and while this has helped some people in releasing weight, it has also caused a few deaths.

1. Essential Supplements

Molybdenum

Molybdenum can stop yeast buildup. Yeast requires special mention as it relates to weight release. An overabundance of yeast may contribute to asthma, weakness, headaches, fatigue, and last but not least, weight gain!

When people are too critical or resentful toward themselves or others, they may have a yeast problem. Antibiotics can cause yeast infections. Yeast in the colon affects the sinuses.

Intuitively, yeast looks like a dusty, misty, or cloudy energy in the body. I have found that many people who are overweight have a high amount of yeast in their system.

Yeast creates acetaldehyde, which is a waste product. Broken down in the body slowly, it can end up stored in fat cells. As people begin to release weight, they will have a die-off

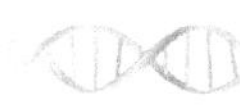

of yeast and the acetaldehyde will be released into the body. The liver can then become overwhelmed and have a difficult time clearing the toxin from the system. The acetaldehyde can get into the brain, bloodstream, joints, and lungs, and impair the memory. So the first thing that the body does is send the message to the brain to stop exercising!

A molybdenum supplement is very beneficial here as it helps to flush the acetaldehyde from the system by turning it into uric acid. A suggestion is to use 300 mcgs at first, move up to 500 mcgs for a few months, and then discontinue use and consider using it again later. The molybdenum will keep your mind clear and prevent brain fog, as well as enable the acetaldehyde to be flushed from the body.

Yeast is attracted to and held by anger and resentment issues, so download:

- 'I know what it feels like to be in a loving environment.'
- 'I know what it feels like to be appreciated.'
- 'I know how to live my life without resenting others and myself.'
- 'I know what it feels like to understand what a person thinks and feels.'
- 'I know it is safe to see intuitively in the body.'
- 'I know what it feels like to witness intuitive changes in yeast and fungus.'

It is not advised to intuitively command all the yeast in a person's body to die. The body needs a certain amount of yeast to function, so do consult your physician before taking molybdenum.

Yeast craves sugars, and an abundance of sugars is what it needs to survive in the body. So people who have yeast problems should consider an alkaline diet because this will starve the yeast of sugars.

Omega 3s

To help release weight, it is very important to take omega 3 fatty acids every day, as they help break down the bad form of cholesterol. It is important to understand that you have to have cholesterol to survive. What happens is that people often eat too much meat and fried food, so they have more bad cholesterol in their system than good.

Omega 3s also allow us to use serotonin, which lifts the mood. So omega 3s will keep you from being depressed as you exercise and your hormone levels move up and down.

Omega 3s can also help keep your skin and hair healthy.

Most of the omega 3s that you get from the store come from fish oil. This comes from the ocean and can contain mercury, so other sources should also be considered. Avocados are high in omega 3s, as are wild rice, walnuts, canola oil (rapeseed oil), flaxseeds, soybeans, and other foods.

Omega 3 (and a little 6) is also in flaxseed oil. Flaxseed oil comes from the seeds of the plant *Linum usitatissimum*, which is a very rich source of alpha linolenic acid. The Mediterranean diet is high in alpha linolenic acid, and it seems to lower the risk of coronary artery disease and certain types of cancer.

It has been indicated in studies that flaxseed oil may help with arteriosclerosis, help prevent heart attacks and strokes,

 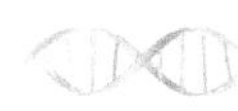

and ease the symptoms of arthritis. It may also be beneficial with some cancers.

Some poultry farmers have begun to feed their chickens a diet rich in flaxseed, boosting the omega 3 fatty acids in the eggs to the point where they are eight to ten times that found in regular eggs. This new kind of holistic thinking has finally reached our farmers!

With regard to releasing weight, the good fat in flaxseed oil helps convert the bad fat from foods and the fat that is still in your body. It is used to treat hardening of the arteries, and can benefit the heart and make the skin beautiful.

One tablespoon of flaxseed oil with cottage cheese is said to produce interferon, which boosts the immune system.

Flaxseed oil has a small amount of omega 6 in it, so women with certain cancers and women who have had cancer should ask their doctors before using it. The omega 6 in flaxseed oil can delay menopause in some women.

It is always best to prevent your oils from going rancid by keeping them refrigerated whenever possible.

Apple Cider Vinegar

Apple cider vinegar is made from ripe apples that are fermented and go through a strict process to create the final product. The vinegar contains a host of vitamins, beta-carotene, and pectin, and vital minerals such as potassium, sodium, magnesium, calcium, phosphorous, chlorine, sulfur, iron, and fluorine. All the health benefits of organic apple cider vinegar are attributed to the presence of these nutrients.

To get the full benefits, make sure that you use only the natural, organic variety of apple cider vinegar. The vinegar will have a

brown color and the 'mother' of the supplement floating on the bottom.

Apple cider vinegar contains a significant amount of pectin, and this has been known to help in regulating blood pressure and reducing bad cholesterol in the body.

Apple cider vinegar is also laden with potassium, so it is used for the treatment of a variety of ailments including hair loss, weak fingernails, brittle teeth, sinusitis, and a permanently running nose.

The beta-carotene in apple cider vinegar may help slow the damage caused by free radicals, helping to maintain a firmer skin and a youthful appearance.

It is claimed that apple cider vinegar is helpful in ailments such as constipation, headaches, arthritis, weak bones, indigestion, high cholesterol, diarrhea, eczema, sore eyes, chronic fatigue, mild food poisoning, hair loss, high blood pressure, and obesity, along with many others. It is good for those who want to release weight, as it may help facilitate weight reduction by supporting the breakdown of fat.

It is said that the best time to drink this vinegar is first thing in the morning. A suggestion is to mix two tablespoons each of apple cider vinegar and honey in a glass of water and drink it.

Apple cider vinegar helps keep your lymph system clear and is as important as the omega 3s in a weight-reduction program. A teaspoon in a glass of water every day will help to clean up the lymph system when you are dropping weight.

You can use apple cider vinegar for as long as you want to, since the overall health benefits have been documented for

over a century in the alternative sector. However, prolonged use is not recommended, as apple cider vinegar is hard on the enamel of the teeth. A three-month on, three-month off regimen is best.

Alpha Lipoic Acid (ALA)

Alpha lipoic acid helps you keep strong and helps your liver produce glutathione, an amino acid that helps pull toxins out of the body and gives you energy. How this works is that the mitochondria in the cell hold all the energy of the cell, which is called ATP. They release the ATP when we need energy. However, when the ATP is released, a small amount of oxygen is released as well, as a waste product. It is called a free radical. Oxygen is very hard on the body if it is not in the right context. So, in order to counter the negative effects of free radicals, the body attaches antioxidants to them. ALA helps to make the antioxidants.

ALA has also been shown to be effective in helping people with diabetes as it can help maintain blood glucose levels.

ALA is available from plant and animal sources. I suggest using it for the first few weeks of your weight-release program – or maybe for the rest of your life! It should be taken with flaxseed oil. That acts as a carrier, ensuring that the ALA is absorbed into the cells.

2. Important Supplements

Lecithin

Lecithin is a lipid that consists of choline and inositol. It is one of the main components within cell membranes. It is an omega 6 fatty acid and has many functions, not least of which is controlling the number of nutrients that flow in and out of the cells.

Lecithin occurs naturally in soya beans, yeast, peanuts, fish, and the yolks of eggs. It is an active ingredient in many weight-loss supplements, either in powder form, in tablets, or as a main ingredient in some shakes, but there is little scientific proof that it helps. There is, however, documentation that supports the theory that the presence of lecithin in the bloodstream may help to prevent atherosclerosis and heart disease. It is the ability of lecithin to assist with keeping fat in the blood solvent that is the reasoning behind claims that the consumption of products containing soya decreases the chances of developing heart disease. The lecithin contained in most supplements has its origin in soya beans.

Lecithin helps your whole body. It keeps the arteries open, helps men to keep their energy up, and boosts sex drive. It is beneficial for veins and arteries, but it is not a complete must in a weight-release plan. Those with any form of cancer should consult their doctor before using it.

Resveratrol

Resveratrol is a substance that occurs in most plants to some degree but is most concentrated in grapevines. It is higher in red wine than in white. This is due to the fact that both the skins and seeds of the grapes are used in the preparation of red wine. In white wine, only the juice is used. Resveratrol is thought to be one of the factors that accounts for the French paradox, which is the finding that coronary heart disease is lower in France, where red wine is often drunk, than in other industrialized countries.

Resveratrol is used in herbal remedies the world over. As well as protecting the cardiovascular system, it is thought it may guard against cancer.

Resveratrol supplements are made from red wine and actually taste good! The reason why I suggest taking them is because if you want to drop weight quickly, you need to make sure you have plenty of antioxidants and a healthy cardiovascular system. Resveratrol also helps with detoxifying the body, as it can keep you strong and give you energy.

Amino Acid Complex

Amino acid complex is something that you might want to look into because it can help to build muscle. I think that it is important to use an amino acid complex when you are releasing weight because it builds your energy and makes you feel stronger

3. *Optional Supplements*

DHEA

DHEA is a steroid hormone that is produced naturally in the body. It is thought by some that when our levels of DHEA are low, we are more susceptible to aging and disease. In a study carried out in 1986 and published in the *New England Journal of Medicine*, it was found that a 100 mcg per deciliter increase in DHEA blood levels corresponded with a 48 percent reduction in death due to cardiovascular disease and a 36 percent reduction in mortality for any reason.

The effect of oral DHEA varies from person to person; however, in a double-blind study, 24 women using DHEA showed noticeable improvement in overall well-being in that they were less depressed at the end of the study.

Supplementation with DHEA can be an aid in weight release. DHEA can stimulate the adrenals, and many doctors prescribe it to help the adrenals recover from periods of prolonged stress. It is also used to promote the production of testosterone. Because of this, differing doses are recommended for men and women. Dosages of 50 mcg for a woman and 100 mcg for a man are suggested. It is best to taper off DHEA slowly, so that the body starts producing cortisone naturally again.

DHEA is optional for weight release and should only be used if you have not had any female cancers.

DHEA supplements are produced and sold legally in the USA. However, due to concerns about potentially serious side effects, including heart palpitations, they are not approved for use in a number of other countries, including the UK and Canada.

Grapefruit Extract

Grapefruit supplements are available in three different types, each claiming a different health benefit. Each is an extract from a different part of the grapefruit: rind extract, seed extract, and whole fruit extract. Grapefruit-extract supplements are available in powder and capsule form, and grapefruit-seed extract is also sold in a liquid form.

The whole grapefruit supplement is the newest supplement of its kind and encompasses extractions from the rinds, seeds, and juice combined. Conjecture about the positive association between grapefruit and weight reduction has circulated for

many years – it is thought to help burn calories, curb appetite, and control feelings of hunger.

So, grapefruit extract is suggested as a part of a weight-release program, but watch for contraindications with medication!

Cactus Juice

Cactus-juice concentrate comes from the prickly pear plant and is said to provide daily dietary and nutritional support for a variety of health concerns. Many nutritionists, herbalists, and medical practitioners are also recognizing the herbal benefits of the prickly pear fruit and nopal cactus.

Cactus juice is a great source of antioxidants; it may have inflammation-fighting capabilities, and it has been shown to lower cholesterol and blood sugars. Some studies have indicated that cactus juice can help diabetes, hyperglycemia, inflammation, high cholesterol, atherosclerosis, colon cleansing, gastrointestinal disorders, and liver function.

Noni

Noni is the Hawaiian name for *Morinda citrifolia*, known as Indian mulberry. The plant is a type of evergreen bush-tree with fruit the size of a potato. The fruit juice is in demand in alternative medicine for many different kinds of illnesses, including arthritis, diabetes, high blood pressure, muscle aches and pains, menstrual difficulties, headaches, heart disease, AIDS, cancers, gastric ulcers, sprains, mental depression, senility, poor digestion, atherosclerosis, blood vessel problems, and drug addiction. Noni is receiving attention from modern herbalists, medical physicians, and high-tech biochemists, and scientific studies within the last few decades have lent support to the claims of its properties. Scientific evidence of the benefits of the noni fruit's juice is limited, but there is some evidence for successful treatment of colds and influenza.

You can introduce noni immediately into the regimen because it's not a harsh parasite cleanse. It does clean out an enormous number of parasites, however. It doesn't stop tapeworms, but it will help with the worms that you may get from the tropics.

Note: If you start to take supplements every day and then suddenly quit using them for no apparent reason, you have run into a belief that needs to be investigated.

Blessing the Supplements You Take

When you buy herbs, vitamins, or any type of food from the store, ask the Creator of All That Is if what you are buying is for your highest and best. You can determine this by connecting to the Creator while holding the product and simply asking if the potency is correct or if the substance is for your highest and best. Energy testing and pendulums are often not useful here, because the subconscious mind has a tendency to interfere with the answer. It's always best to ask the Creator.

Once the substance has passed the test, it should be blessed before use to ensure maximum potency, effectiveness, and quality. Since everything has a consciousness and we absorb this essence when we consume it, we need to bless all the food and herbs we eat! If these substances have not been treated with the respect they deserve, the benefits of eating them will be reduced.

This includes downloading your prescription medication with a blessing. Do not hate your medication; bless it, and your supplements, in the following way:

How to Bless Medication and Supplements

- Center yourself in your heart, and visualize going down into Mother Earth, which is a part of All That Is.
- Visualize bringing up energy through your feet, opening each chakra to the crown chakra. In a beautiful ball of light, go out to the universe.
- Go beyond the universe, past the layers of lights, past the golden light, past the jellylike substance that is the Laws, into a pearly iridescent snow-white light, into the Seventh Plane of Existence.
- Make the command: *'Creator of All That Is, it is commanded that this medicine that I take be blessed from when it was made into the present and forward into the future. May it be blessed with the ability to be absorbed into my body to give me the best effect, without the side effects. Thank you. It is done. It is done. It is done.'*
- Imagine the energy coming down into your space through every cell of your body.
- When you have finished, connect back to the energy of All That Is, take a deep breath in, and make an energy break if you so choose.

PARASITES

When I was a little girl, I could never get up in the morning, and I was always tired – and skinny. My mom would say to me and my sister, 'You girls must have tapeworms! You are just too skinny.'

Do you know what parasites do? They do make you really skinny at first. In fact, in the 1920s, actors and actresses would get tapeworms on purpose to stay skinny. But then what happens is the body starts to think it's starving and it starts to store fat.

My mother was right: my sister and I did have tapeworms. I assume that I got them because I went barefoot all the time. Finally, about 20 years ago, when I went on my first lemon cleanse, I passed a three-foot tapeworm. After that, I was able to wake up in the mornings, and suddenly I began to be able to recognize parasites in my human relationships.

Once I noticed that one of the students who came to take my summer classes was skinny to the point of being unhealthy. I felt that he had parasites and suggested that he use protein shakes, take vitamins and, most important of all, go on a parasite cleanse using noni juice. He did so, and gained back almost 30 pounds (66 kg), and all his muscle and strength.

Parasites can do two things: they can make you too skinny or make you gain a lot of weight, but it always shifts to heavy in the end because your body thinks it's starving, so it holds on to the fat.

Parasites can also get into the colon and leave a lot of acidic residue. Your body knows that it can't live with that much acid,

and it will try to pull it out and encapsulate it in fat cells. This is because the body knows that it has to maintain an alkaline balance to stay alive.

In this way, parasite infections can cause obesity. People have been known to release 10–20 pounds (4.5–9 kg) of weight just from a simple herbal parasite cleanse. So often people who are even slightly overweight will have parasites. Even healthy people who aren't over- or underweight should probably do a parasite cleanse at least once a year.

It is interesting that when I tell people that they may be overweight because of parasites, it changes how they view themselves. Instead of blaming themselves, they begin to think that a parasite is the reason they are so heavy, and, maybe for the first time in their lives, they start investigating the possibility and taking steps to make changes in their life.

Parasites can come in two ways:

1. As microbes (little tiny things and long worms and bacteria).

2. As people who attach themselves to you in a less than savory way and/or take a lot of your energy.

The removal of the 'parasite energy' in your life can make a big difference to your ability to release weight.

Parasite Cleanses

A parasite cleanse can be done in three ways:

1. By going to the doctor to get checked.

2. By doing belief work to release the programs that allow parasites to attach themselves to you.

3. By doing an herbal parasite cleanse.

Truly, all three may be in order. During an herbal parasite cleanse, beliefs and feelings may come up to be cleared. It is best to do belief work on any parasitical programs that you may have relating to weight.

The questions to ask yourself are:

- 'Who are the parasitical people in my life?'
- 'Whom do I resent?'

Looking at who these people are and why you feel you have to keep them in your life will bring out the underlying belief and programs.

It is necessary to recognize that parasites influence us on more than a physical level. They are drawn to the thought processes and feelings that block our development on all levels: physically, emotionally, mentally, and spiritually. Thoughts and feelings such as *I must allow others to take advantage of me* and *I must allow people to suck me dry* are a magnet to parasites. People with parasites have self-esteem issues.

When we do belief work and feeling work, we are freed from the programs that attract parasites. As we remove, replace, and add feelings from the Creator to ourselves with the belief work, we will gain the strength to expel parasites from the inner body as well as from the outer body. Parasites cannot

survive in or around a body that doesn't have the programs that attract them.

Downloads to Repel Parasites

- 'I know how to live without being sucked dry.'
- 'I know how to say no.'
- 'I know when to say no.'
- 'I know I am connected to the Creator at all times.'
- 'I know the difference between the feelings of my parasites and my own feelings.'
- 'I know when I am too tired to do something.'
- 'I know I can live my life without having to be a martyr.'
- 'I know how to live without giving up all my time and effort to please someone else.'
- 'I know the person I have to please is the Creator of All That Is.'
- 'I know how to put good food in my body.'
- 'I know how to command my body to have the proper pH balance.'

We do not intuitively command all parasites to leave the body, as some parasitical bacteria help digest food and it is normal to have them, but in any case you would not be allowed to do this because you are spiritually protected from doing things like this to yourself.

Herbal and Dietary Suggestions to Eliminate Parasites

Suggested parasite cleanses for tapeworms and flukes (with the advice of a qualified health practitioner):

- Cayenne pepper
- Cloves
- Garlic
- Ginger
- Ionic copper
- Noni juice or seeds
- Oregano oil (this can be hard on the stomach, so put 2 drops in capsules)
- Pumpkin seeds or pumpkin-seed extract
- The fresh juice of 2 carrots, 1 stick of celery, and ½ beet (beetroot), together with a little garlic and a pinch of ginger
- Walnut/wormwood combination (this should not be used by diabetics)

General suggestions:

- Charcoal (this kills giardia and other parasites)
- Colloidal silver (this kills yeast and all kinds of parasites, but taking it all the time isn't recommended)
- Colloidal platinum (kills yeast and all kinds of parasites)

- Thyme (this kills parasites in drinking water)
- Make the body alkaline (*see pages 101–102*). If the body has an alkaline balance of 7.2 to 7.4, parasites will have a difficult time surviving.
- Use a herbal parasite cleanse in the spring (not in winter, because then the body is in a rest period). Doing several parasite cleanses in succession is very hard on the body, so discernment is in order. If it is found that a herbal cleanse is needed, follow this process: ten days on, five days off, ten days on, five days off, ten days on, five days off, so you can destroy all the eggs laid by the parasite.

If you do a parasite cleanse, it is best to balance it with an alkaline diet so that the process isn't so emotional. The 'feelings' you will experience during a cleanse may not be your own. Feelings like 'I'm going to die,' are coming from the consciousness of the parasites and worms that are dying.

Ridding yourself of parasites also helps you to let go of emotional parasites (people who suck you dry) and 'energetic parasites,' such as waywards, spiritual hooks, etc.

Food Program to Avoid Parasites

All meats and vegetables have some parasites attached to them. Regardless, the more balanced your belief systems are, the fewer parasites you will pick up.

To avoid parasites, it is essential to avoid overeating and to chew all food thoroughly. This allows food to be digested properly and facilitates the absorption of nutrients. Parasites thrive in the damp conditions often created by inadequately digested foods.

Eat foods with bitter, hot, and sour flavors, as these assist the body in eliminating parasites.

Choose foods that repel parasites. The following have anti-parasitic properties:

- *Beneficial vegetables:* beets (beetroot), cabbage, carrots, garlic, leeks, onion, radishes, and sorrel.
- *Helpful spices:* fennel, cloves, cayenne, garden sage, ginger, horseradish, and thyme.
- *Additional helpful foods:* almonds (use sparingly), kelp, and umeboshi plums. Pumpkin seeds are especially helpful, as they destroy parasites. Raw pumpkin seeds can be eaten as snacks.

5

Weight Release Step 3: The Heart Song

In July 2006, as I related in *Advanced ThetaHealing*, I began to feel extremely fatigued. Thinking that my lungs were the problem, I began to do healings on them. While I was in the process of one of these healings, the voice of the Creator came into my head and asked, 'What are you doing?'

I replied, 'I am working on my lungs.'

The Creator said, 'It isn't your lungs. You have congestive heart failure.'

In utter despair I cried, 'That's impossible! I am too young.'

To be sure, I made an appointment with the doctor. After putting me through some tests, he said, 'You have congestive heart failure. I am so sorry.'

I asked, 'What am I supposed to do about it? How is it healed?'

The doctor said, 'Try this medicine and see if it works. Since you are young, we can put your name on a waiting list for a heart transplant.'

In this moment of desolation I cried to myself, 'Not again! Once more a doctor is telling me that I am going to die.' I went into the 'poor me' abyss. What really upset me about the whole situation was that I had done so much belief work and now I knew I had to do more.

I started taking the medicine, thinking, 'Well, I've promised to go and do the next ThetaHealing seminar. I must keep my promise.'

About two weeks before I left for Rome, where I was due to do the seminar, I had some guests over to my house. They were professional musicians from New York who were taking my Intuitive Anatomy class. They had come to have dinner and play some music. One of them played a magnificent viola, and the sound that came from this instrument was full of melancholy and pulled at the heartstrings.

The other musician asked me to help him compose some music. He told me to sing the music I had in my heart. I went up and connected to the Seventh Plane and began to sing in a mournful tone, feeling a strange emotion coming from my heart. As I felt these energies being lifted from me through the tone I was singing, I suddenly saw all the reasons for my unhappiness and the reasons for my sickness. I realized that I was holding old sorrows in the molecules of my heart. I had always worked on my beliefs without thinking of setting my heart free from the ancient pains it was holding on to. That was why I had continued to feel a sort of unmovable sufferance in my heart. I closed my eyes and let all this sadness come out in a tone that came from my heart. I continued to hold this tone until I was out of breath, and then I started over again.

When I had finished and the music stopped, I opened my eyes and saw that the people in the room were crying. At that

moment, I realized that I had found a way for others to melt the pain and the suffering in their hearts, too.

There is more to the story, but in essence, my heart was healed.

Afterward, I began to release weight. I lost 2 pounds (0.9 kg) every other day until I had released over 30 pounds (13.6 kg). I believe that this is because I released the sadness I had been carrying.

You may never need to do this exercise, but if you feel you don't want to do it, you probably need to do it.

In the exercise, you are going to go up and ask the Creator to release all the sorrow and sadness that is no longer serving you, or which you no longer want to keep. But you are also going to release something else: the pure frustration of every lifetime of attempting to wake the world up and failing. (You should download the knowing that you will succeed this time.)

When you were born, you came in on a special grid system. Not only did you pick the time of your birth, you picked how the stars would line up. This is so you could achieve everything you came to learn. There are no mistakes in the universe. You picked the very moment of arrival, and when you arrived, you came through the emotional energy of this world. Every crying mother, every sad moment, that has happened on this Earth was recorded in your body. So, when you release this sorrow, you aren't just releasing it from yourself and the land, but also releasing it from your genetics, your ancestors, and your past lives. You are releasing it from each of your organs. The heart song is a Sixth-Plane exercise using vibration to heal and reset the body.

The Heart Song

This process is to release sorrow and anger from all levels through a continuous tone that comes from the heart and is re-created by the voice.

The practitioner should guide the clients through the process. Only the voice of the clients is able to release the sorrow and pain in their heart. The practitioner cannot release it for them and can only assist them by encouraging them to create the tone in the following way:

- Center yourself in your heart and visualize going down into Mother Earth, which is part of All That Is.
- Visualize bringing up energy through your feet, opening each chakra to the crown chakra. In a beautiful ball of light, go out into the universe.
- Go beyond the universe, past the layers of lights, past the golden light, past the jellylike substance that is the Laws, into a pearly iridescent snow-white light, into the Seventh Plane of Existence.
- Make the command: *'Creator of All That Is, I command that sorrow is released from the heart through a tone from my voice. Thank you. It is done. It is done. It is done.'*
- Imagine that you are going down deep into your heart. Listen to the sad song your heart is singing.

Let the tone come out in your voice. It will not be loud, but a steady, neutral tone. If you 'shout out' the sorrow, it pulls it all back in, so just release it slowly through an even tone.

- As you listen to the sound, listen to all the resentments, the frustrations with war, famine, hatred, and anger that have been locked in your heart. Let the sound of the heart come out of your mouth.
- Do this with every organ in your body, moving from the heart to the solar plexus and then the stomach, and from there as you choose. If you are feeling exhausted, however, start in your adrenals and kidneys, so you can get some energy moving through your body. Concentrate on releasing the energy from each organ until you are sure it has gone, and then move on to the next one.
- Remember, you aren't just doing this for yourself, but for your family, too. When people start to release sadness for the first time, often they want to run. Remember, you need to finish this process for your family.
- When you've finished, connect back to the energy of All That Is, take a deep breath in, and make an energy break if you so choose.

The way to tell that the process has finished is that you feel it has finished. You will feel as though you have released all the built-up sorrow and anger from your heart and other organs and will be left feeling energized and joyful.

This process may be done more than once if you need to release your sorrow in layers.

If you are working with clients and they don't feel comfortable releasing all the stored sorrow with another person, they can continue the process when they are alone.

One of my students took four days to feel as though she had finished the process. I took about six hours for my whole body.

Interestingly, most people who need to lose weight will release a lot of energy from the solar plexus, which is where the pain of losing children and other family members is held, and from the throat area, which is where there can be problems with the thyroid when you don't express yourself, aren't able to express yourself, or over-express yourself. Most healers I meet have a little block right in the thyroid, because they are afraid of hurting other people's feelings.

RELEASING THE SADNESS

Sadness from the Family

When teaching a class, I can always pick out the people who have been selected to carry the energetic burdens of their family. Generally, they are a little bit heavier than other members of the family and have a messy house as well. How you keep your house is a reflection of your beliefs, genetic or otherwise. If your house is cluttered, you have too much genetic clutter inside as well. In western society, this is always more prevalent through the holidays.

We all have perceived images of ourselves and others and have a tendency to play roles in the family to fit those images. Some people believe, for example, that if they are grandparents, they have to be huggable. 'Grandmas have to be fat.' By now you will realize that if you have that belief, some belief work is in order.

Also, as we have already discussed, in ancient societies the people who were heavier were the respected ones. So, depending on your DNA and genetics, your body may be attempting to gain respect, even if it is from ten generations back. Everything that is happening in your body is for a purpose, even if it seems that it isn't for your highest and best at the time.

Releasing your own sadness will release the energetic burdens of your family, too.

Sadness from the Land

When you release sadness with the heart song, it releases it from the land as well. This is because you may be carrying in your DNA the residue of what has happened in your country. If your country has ever been the site of a war, for instance, there may be a lot of grief to be released. In fact, we have all lost people in war somewhere back in our ancestry. We may not remember it, but our grandparents might, or our parents. It may not be that long ago. This sadness can be released with the heart song.

If you have moved from your home country, the heart song will release sadness both from where you were born and from where you live now. Once you have lived in a place for seven years, you will start to pick up on the emotional vibrations of that area, and this will include some of the sadness.

Even if you release the sadness when visiting a country that is not your own, it will help both your own land and the one you are in. This is why I started telling my teachers to do this process everywhere they went – and why we did it in class when I went to Germany.

I found that Germany and many other parts of Europe hadn't recovered from the devastation of World War II – the emotions were still there. The sadness from that time pervaded much of the land and was there in the people, as it is also in the Jewish people and in some of the people in Japan.

Similarly, when you go to the southern states in the USA, you find they still haven't recovered from the Civil War. The sadness from those days is still in the land and still in the people. If you go to places where Civil War battles took place, you can psychically see soldiers still fighting in the fields.

Any form of pain or suffering will leave its mark on the land and its people. I once worked on an African-American man who was a Baptist minister and had issues with the black slaves of the USA. As you know, when European people started moving into the Americas, they brought black slaves with them. Not everyone treated these slaves badly, and at the time it was normal for people to have slaves. Some of the Southern plantation owners treated their slaves better than others, considering the time and place. However, this man was filled with the grief and anger of the slave trade. For him, it was as if it had happened yesterday. Through the heart song, he released this feeling from his genetics, his history, and probably from the land that he was raised in, and when he had finished, I could see in his eyes that relief and joy had replaced the sadness. He was ready to move forward with his life.

It is important to be aware of the energy that will come from the land and its people. You can talk to people from where I live in Idaho, for instance, and they'll say you have to be tough to live in Idaho. It's true, because we have really cold winters, and this land was settled by people who had nothing and had to be strong to live here. I call the place 'settler land' and the attitude 'settler mentality.' You should see the land out in Roberts. I used to live in a place that was plagued by mosquitoes, flies, heat, mice, spiders, and the smell of cows, and if you said anything to anyone out there about the conditions, they would tell you to 'cowboy up.' You still have to be tough to live in Idaho, and if you don't like it, you can just go back where you came from! So, what is the energy of the land? Be strong, be tough.

Ask yourself, what has gone on in your land? Do you have any idea of how your ancestors lived? What battles went on there? What betrayals took place? In America, the English settlers made peace with the Native Americans and then turned around and took their land. The Netherlands and British Isles had some crazy things happen! What about Russia? What is the legacy of that land? Do you have to be strong to live in Russia?

But what if you didn't have to carry the hardship of your ancestors? Well, you don't have to carry it. With the heart song, you can clear the sadness of your ancestors even in the spirit world.

The reason for this is that the heart song is directly connected to the collective consciousness of humankind. With this process, we release the suffering of all humankind. Many of the people who do this exercise will connect to the universal tone that releases anger, hatred, and sorrow on a universal level, and this will benefit us all.

6

Weight Release Step 4: Bless Your Food, Bless Your Body, Less Is Better

One day I asked, 'God, why am I overweight?' As always, the Creator answered me patiently. I was told, 'Vianna, you have a resilient body. You should bless your body. Encourage your body, don't discourage it. Bless it. Blessings are stronger than curses.'

This led me to consider the relationship between body and mind.

BODY AND MIND

'Food is Bad...'

Do you know your own body? Do you know how big your stomach is? Have you ever touched your own stomach and actually said hello to it?

One of the first things you should consider, if you are overweight, is becoming acquainted with your intestinal tract. This starts when your food goes into your mouth. How do you feel about your food?

What happens to some people is they develop a hatred of food and of their own body. For instance, if they compulsively eat a lot of food at one sitting, they may become angry with themselves afterward and wish they hadn't done it. When they do this, they affect the body's ability to break down the food and convert it into energy properly. This is because the body is getting mixed messages. What can happen at this point is that all that food is converted into fat. So, if you don't love yourself and you think food is bad, not only may you actually be stopping part of your digestive process, but you may also be making yourself fat.

Go easy on yourself – if you have craved something and then eaten it, in many instances this will be because your body needed it at that moment. Trust your body – don't be angry with it.

It is said that people who are overweight have hormones that don't work correctly and don't send the signal to their stomach that they are full and should stop eating. I'm not sure if I believe this, but I do know that there are several reasons why some people eat all the time:

In order to feel present in this reality. Some people live too much in the future and need to be in the now, spiritually, mentally, and physically.

Because they are hungry. This may be because their food has no nutritional value. As a consequence, their body sends the signal that it needs more food in order to get the nutrition it needs and the person ends up eating all the time and gaining weight.

Because their body cannot absorb the nutrients from their food because they have parasites. Parasites can make people

hungrier, too. A parasite cleanse might be indicated (*see pages 75–80*).

Because they are sitting in front of the television eating potato chips! Many people say they eat more when they do this. Many of the quality chips are cooked in omega 3s now, so it's not such a detrimental practice as it once was, but it's still not recommended.

What's interesting is that most people who are overweight don't eat all the time. In fact, the reason why some are heavy is that they only eat once a day and then they gorge. It is better to eat three carefully planned meals a day and two snacks than one huge meal.

People who are obese due to medication also have a tendency to skip regular nutritious meals. Fruit and vegetables are a must for these people, as they need something to clean the intestinal tract.

Food Is What You Make It!

In itself, eating is not bad. Where would we be without it? For most of us, eating the right foods will actually help with weight release.

What is healthy food? Why exactly is it healthy? It is because we think that it is good for us. Our mind plays a far larger role than we may realize. Have you ever eaten a piece of chocolate cake and then felt guilty that you ate it? Now the chocolate cake has a consciousness all its own, and a message has been sent with it into your body. Now your body doesn't reach for the nutrients that are in the cake because you have just told it that

the cake is toxic, and the body is intelligent – more intelligent than science acknowledges. So it will reject the nutrients, but take all the toxins from the cake and encapsulate those toxins in fat cells.

To take another example: to the alternative way of thinking, white sugar is a poison, but so is everything in excess. You actually eat a pile of sugar each year (mostly without knowing it) and don't die as a result. Get out of the thinking that white sugar (in moderation) is toxic. Don't get me wrong – too much of anything is toxic, and too much white sugar isn't good. But we all eat some white sugar and our body copes just fine.

What I do believe is toxic in small amounts is artificial sweeteners like saccharine and Nutra-sweet. I believe that these are much more difficult for the body to process than white sugar, and they may be carcinogens.

The American Cancer Society once found that people who used artificial sweeteners actually gained weight instead of losing it. Artificial sweeteners are far worse than regular sugar on the body. Stevia, on the other hand, seems to be a non-toxic artificial sweetener and can be used as an alternative to sugar. And *chocolate*, used judiciously, can actually aid weight release, just as I predicted years ago.

The key is to learn to work with your body. It is doing its best to serve you. If you get up in the middle of the night and crave a potato chip, this means that your body needs something. It is up to you to go up and ask God what that something is.

What is important is to reach a point where you are absorbing your food properly, and then you won't need as much. You will absorb it if you stop hating it and hating your body. Download:

- 'I am becoming the perfect me.'
- 'My body is strong.'
- 'I am beautiful.'
- 'I am healthy.'

THE HAZARDS OF DIETING

If you go on a diet, the first thing you lose is water. You may lose 10 pounds (4.5 kg), but it will all be in water. As soon as your body loses this water weight, it automatically goes into panic and fights to hold on to the fat. Even if you cut back your food consumption to just a tiny piece of lettuce a day, your body will hold on to its fat and not release it. It does this so that in a moment of crisis, it can release the fat to be used. It will release muscle before it releases fat because fat has more value in a time of crisis. And if you are eating only tiny portions of food, your body will assume that it needs to prepare for a crisis.

Unfortunately, in any event, the concept of 'going on a diet' has negative programs attached to it. Many of us fail to realize this when we start out, but we end up feeling that we are depriving ourselves of nourishment that we are commonly used to, instead of embracing the plan as a positive experience.

The worst thing with a diet is that you may lose weight while you are on it, but as soon as you go back to your old diet, you gain it all back. It can seem that you're getting nowhere. I know people who get so tired of being on a diet that they go on binges and eat like crazy.

I once read in a magazine that someone had created a diet pill that would stop a person from absorbing carbohydrates. I was immediately dubious. Do you know what a carbohydrate is? It is one of the five things that make up your body. These are:

1. Carbohydrates (sugars)

2. Lipids (oils)

3. Protein, a complex energy that breaks down into sugar that your body uses to make…

4. ATP, and of course the other thing is…

5. DNA (nucleic acid).

So, obviously, you have to have carbohydrates to live. Why would you take a pill to prevent your body from absorbing them? That isn't likely to be good for you.

A little bit of advice is to stop counting calories and begin to count carbohydrates. A meal consisting of steak, a baked potato, and a serving of vegetables converts to just over 35 carbohydrates, and this is with butter on the potato, whereas just one Coca-Cola has a whopping 45 carbohydrates in it! This is why we should choose the right kind of sugars and the right kind of diet. For instance, potatoes are good for you, in spite of the hype that they are fattening. They have more vitamins and minerals than many other foods. And margarine is much worse for you than butter on that potato, folks!

VEGETARIAN AND OTHER DIETS

There are a lot of diets out there, and it's true that people who eat only protein are thinner than other folks, but some people can actually diet themselves into aggression. Low-cholesterol

 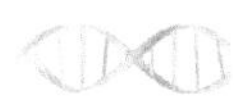

diets such as the all-protein diet (a diet low in omegas) may cause aggressive behavior.

I teach a lot of vegetarians, and half of them are overweight. Many of them don't know how to be vegetarian and go through life deficient in protein. So, when it is time to do some heavy lifting, their strength is depleted. It is imperative for the budding vegetarian to learn to follow a healthy diet plan.

As for vegans, smart ones know they have to have protein, so they eat beans, avocados, and other fruit and vegetables that have protein in them.

As already mentioned, an alkaline diet will make the body uninhabitable to parasites – and that goes for bacteria, viruses, fungi, and other microbes, too. The body needs to be about 7.2 to 7.4 alkaline to resist parasites, yeast, bacteria, and other challenges. It is equipped to fight off viruses, bacteria, and parasites, but if it becomes too acidic, the immune system is stressed and these entities can get out of control. When it is alkaline, on the other hand, every organ will come back into balance.

Cucumbers, spinach, avocados, and other greens are alkaline foods, whereas most types of fruit are acidic.

Mental attitude has a part to play as well. The more positive a person is, the more alkaline the body is. The more negative, the more acidic.

We know this from experience, because when we staged an Intuitive Anatomy class in Hawaii once, we cleared so many issues from the students that by the end of the three weeks, everyone's acid-alkaline balance was 7.2 alkaline – and they were still eating chocolate cake. Belief work made my entire class alkaline in just a short period of time.

In theory, you have to eat alkaline-based food to keep your alkalinity at 7.2, and then nothing can make you sick. However, I have had clients come to me who are completely alkaline but are still sick. I have found that the reason for this is that they haven't cleared their resentment and anger.

I am not attempting to steer you to one diet over another. What I am telling you to do is to bless whatever diet that you go on....

BLESS YOUR FOOD

I know that cell talks to cell, and therefore I know that my cells can talk to your cells. I know that when I look into your space and see things that happened to you as a child. I know that everything on Earth has a memory. So when you eat food, you are picking up all the energy of that food and what it has gone through in its life.

I once had someone explain his rendition of reincarnation to me: a man dies, they bury him, the grass grows, the cow eats the grass, the man shoots the cow and eats it and has the other man's memories. Now I know that it probably doesn't work to that extreme, but I believe that to some extent you do pick up the memories of everything that you put in your mouth. If you were to eat a plant that grew in a healthy, loving, wonderful, and joyful environment, I would assume that you would get healthy, loving, wonderful, and joyful energy from eating it. So I would also assume that if you were to eat an animal that has been kept in captivity, often barbarically treated, you

would get a kind of angry emotion from the food. Have you ever seen what happens to pigs? They are kept as prisoners. Or dairy cows? They are fed and milked and kept as prisoners on farms, and if they get sick, they are put down. And you are eating the cheese and drinking the milk. So I think that when people who have studied Buddhism or Hinduism tell you not to eat certain types of food because it could be your ancestor, there might be something to it, because they know you are getting the essence of the food.

I'm not going to tell you not to eat cows or pigs, but to do something different when you eat: bless your food and bless it from the very beginning; from the time it was born to the time that you eat it, or from the time it was a seed to the time that you eat it. In many instances, particularly since the advent of modern farming, we don't even feed our plants what they need anymore. We give them lots of nitrogen so they look really pretty and green. But plants need more than that – they need vitamins and minerals to grow, just as we do.

Meditation for Blessing Food

- Center yourself in your heart and visualize going down into Mother Earth, which is a part of All That Is.
- Visualize bringing up energy through your feet, opening each chakra to the crown chakra. In a beautiful ball of light, go out to the universe.

- Go beyond the universe, past the layers of lights, past the golden light, past the jellylike substance that is the Laws, into a pearly iridescent snow-white light, into the Seventh Plane of Existence.
- Make the command: *'Creator of All That Is it is commanded that this food that I am about to eat be blessed back to when it was a seed, from the moment it was conceived into the present and forward. May it be blessed with the ability to be absorbed into my body, to give me the highest and best nutrition. May the source from which it comes, be it animal or plant, be blessed and thanked for giving me the energy of life. May the spirit of my brothers and sisters, the plants and animals, be sent to the divine light. It is commanded that everything that I eat be supercharged, that I absorb it and become strong from it. Thank you. It is done. It is done. It is done.'*
- Imagine the energy going into your food.
- When you have finished, connect back to the energy of All That Is, take a deep breath in and make an energy break if you so choose.

LESS IS BETTER

At one time I would go for long periods without eating a lot, or just not eat at all. But, as I found, if you do this, your body will think you are starving to death and you won't release weight.

One guide that works well is the diabetes diet that is covered later in this book (*see page 135*). This is where you only eat 30

 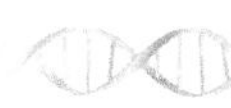

carbohydrates per meal and 15–20 carbohydrates for a snack, but you have to eat three times a day and snack twice a day. One of the strangest things that happened when I followed the diabetes diet is that I was actually eating more.

You should know that people who go without breakfast gain weight. You have to eat something in the morning, and it helps if it has fewer than 30 carbohydrates. In one study, it was found that American teenagers who ate breakfast every day weighed 15 pounds (7 kg) less than those who didn't eat breakfast. One theory is that when people fast and then consume large amounts of food all at once, they have a tendency to store fat, and eventually to become obese.

Small meals that are spaced throughout the day are definitely better for you than consuming large meals all at once. Strict monitoring of the *carbohydrate* consumption (not calories) will help in an overall diet plan.

The diabetes diet of eating 30 carbohydrates per meal and 15–20 carbohydrates in two snacks a day will reduce body weight and lower the blood glucose levels. Carbohydrates are found in foods such as bread, vegetables, fruit, and pasta. Reading labels pertaining to carbohydrates is the key to a proper diet for those who have diabetes. In many instances, diabetes can be improved with exercise and a diet low in carbohydrates. Increasing fiber will help as well.

You can also make a major improvement to your diet just by eliminating all white bread and gluten.

This is all well and good if you don't travel. I do travel and unfortunately because of this, I eat what is available. But I have come up with a solution: I just tell my body, 'Less is better.' So, instead of eating a lot of food, I only eat specific foods and ones I like. If I want a doughnut, I eat one, but I only eat half of it, because less is better. What usually happens is that all of a sudden I'm not hungry halfway through the doughnut, so I don't eat it all.

You should be able to eat what you want, but it is best to download that you get full quickly and that all the nutrition in the food is given to your body and absorbed completely. Also, choose foods that don't have saturated fat in them. Animal fats should be kept to a minimum. However, you should be sure to get adequate protein. Be sure to drink enough water to remain hydrated, too – this is also very important.

I can honestly tell you that nowadays I eat whatever I want to, and I crave foods that are good for me. That is the difference – eating a variety of healthy foods but none to excess. If I allow myself to have a piece of cake, I am also careful not to worry about it, because if I worry too much, then a program is created. Granted, it is likely that I will only take a bite or two of the cake anyway (less is better), but I make sure I don't let myself become overwhelmed with guilt because of those bites.

You can even download 'Less [substance] is better' for people who are trying to beat addictions.

And of course, a good download to give yourself is: 'Less feels better to me.'

Really what you are doing is changing the way you feel about food.

7

Weight Release Step 5: Exercise Without Exercise

Remember the Creator's message to me? 'Vianna, anyone who tells you that you can release weight without exercise is trying to sell you something. You have to exercise! And when you can't exercise every day, your brain has to *think* you are still exercising every day.'

So now I'm going to show you how to release weight using your subconscious mind and God.

Don't think you can lie in bed all day and still drop weight, though. Your body needs to move.

This was bad news for me. I always wanted a piece of equipment that would exercise for me. I love it when machines do chores. I thought the dishwasher was the greatest invention ever! We have washers, dryers, and dishwashers, so why not a machine that exercises for us? But this isn't why we are in a human body: we are in a human body to have an experience through that body, and that means we do need to move from time to time. So first let's look at how to do some real exercise.

RUNNING... THE CORRECT WAY

When I was in nuclear security training, I got in good shape even though I had asthma when I started the course. By the time I finished, I could do 59 push-ups inside a minute, and 57 sit-ups in a minute, and I held the second fastest women's record for running the 'river run' – a two-mile (3.2-km) course in Idaho Falls. This was because I learned how to breathe and move in the right way when running. I will explain that to you later. When I ran, I listened to specific music so I could sing to it, and this helped me with focus. When I listened to the music when I wasn't running, I could envision myself out running again. In any event, when I was in nuclear security training, I ran every day.

Most women run more slowly than men. Biologically, men have different muscle tone in their legs that helps them run faster and longer. Running isn't about who can run faster or longer, however. The only person you should be in competition with is yourself. If you decide that you want to use running for exercise, don't worry about others and what they are doing – focus on yourself.

If you are going to run, there are a few things you should know about the correct way to run. Whenever I see someone jogging, I look to see if they know what they're doing. What I have found while watching joggers all over the world is that most people don't know the correct way to run for exercise.

When people say that running is bad for your legs and bones, it is because of incorrect running and poor equipment. The best equipment you can give yourself is a good running shoe. This makes a big difference when you run. Shoes that are designed

to take up the shock from running are a must, so you should pick the best that your money can buy.

In the military, they sing when they run. The trick is that when you are singing, your lungs don't think they are dying from lack of oxygen. What happens to some people when they first start to run is they try to align their breathing to the steps they are taking. So they breathe more heavily than is necessary and start to hyperventilate. Singing is a perfect way to balance this out. If you sing when you run, this will regulate your breathing. Having someone to talk to while you run will also help you to breathe better.

In the armed forces, they also teach you how to run so that you don't develop 'shin splints.' They do something called a 'shuffle' and they run gently rather than in an all-out sprint like they do in the Olympics.

To run correctly, you should run on the balls of your feet rather than put your heels down first. If you run with your heel hitting the ground before your toe, this will give you shin splints. Instead, you should run on the middle bottom padding of your foot in a shuffling movement, using the balls of your feet to move you forward. You aren't taking giant steps, but light strides which are a lot faster than a normal walk.

A mistake some people make when running long distances is to move their arms up and down rapidly as they run. This isn't the way to run several miles comfortably. The correct way is to leave your hands loose in front of you with your arms tucked at your side, with very little motion to them. This is so you don't burn up a lot of energy through unnecessary movement of your arms. Strangely, with a shuffle, the less you move, the farther you can run.

To this day I still remember what it feels like to run to the inspirational music of the composer Yanni. As soon as I hear his music, I am ready to run, and it's been 20 years since I was in nuclear security training using his music for inspiration. If you have music to distract you, you can run better.

If you run a mile (1.6 km), you will stimulate your heart and circulation. This will help keep your body strong. But when it comes to releasing weight by running, they say the first mile doesn't count. Anything after the first mile, however, and the body begins to burn fat reserves. So you will start dropping weight after the first mile, and if you were to run two or three miles (three to five kilometers) every day, you would lose weight very quickly.

There is a secret behind running: when you finish that first mile, the second mile is a breeze, and it is the same concept on an elliptical machine. When you've done 8 minutes on an elliptical, it's not that hard to do 30. So, don't be overwhelmed by the thought that you have to do 30 minutes of exercise – just take it in small steps. Start with eight minutes and then decide if you want to continue.

STARTING OUT

There will always be people who can't exercise or become active overnight, and if this is you, I suggest using different pieces of machinery to assist you in exercising. There is equipment that can help.

The majority of people, however, are mobile enough for moderate exercise. Those who aren't mobile need to work on their bodies with healings and belief work so they can become mobile. If you have real physical problems and, for example, can't move a certain limb, this requires some special belief work. You also need to make an appointment with a physical therapist to help get your limbs moving. There is equipment for people who cannot move that stimulates the body to get the circulation moving. Unfortunately, I know many people who have bought this equipment and never used it!

However, most people can walk for exercise, even if they can't run. Walking is an excellent start. As with every form of exercise, however, you should quit if you feel intense pain. This doesn't mean the good old muscle soreness that you are supposed to have. There is a difference between muscle soreness and the kind of pain that indicates a torn muscle or a buildup of toxins.

Why Some People Fail

Three days after starting a new exercise regime, some people are going to lose their momentum and put the whole thing off. Do you know how they put it off? They say to themselves, 'Well, when I've eaten this cherry pie I'll have to exercise, but I'll do it tomorrow, because today I'm too tired.'

What does this mean as it relates to the subconscious mind? When you are saying something like this, your subconscious is saying to itself:

'I will start exercising tomorrow, I promise.'
'If tomorrow never comes, I will never have to exercise.'

These are the words and thought-forms that lead to ultimate failure. If they are the first statements to come out of your mouth when you talk about exercise, your subconscious is sabotaging you.

How do you know you are being sabotaged? Because you're putting off starting the new thing in your life. And why? The answer is usually fear.

It isn't fear of being fat. What is it? *Fear of being thin!*

AN ALTERNATIVE METHOD

A long time ago I read an article about an experiment with two basketball teams. One team practiced every day and the other team meditated every other day. While in meditation, they visualized that they were practicing for an hour every day. When the two teams played each other, they found that they were at the same level of competence and played with the same amount of energy. So, apparently, imagining that you are exercising works as well as really exercising. Curious to see if it would work for me, I began to experiment.

Of course you might well think, *Why should I imagine that I am exercising for a half hour when I can just get up and exercise? If I have the time to imagine it, I have the time to actually do it.*

The answer is that many of us truly do not have the time to exercise every day. We need an alternative method to help us to release weight.

So here is what I did: I downloaded the feeling and the knowing from the Creator that whenever I listened to one particular song, my body was exercising.

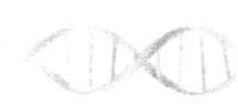

I had used this download method before, to anchor the energy of time slowing down and stretching to the song 'Time Stand Still' by Rush. This was useful when I drove to work. If I played this song, it seemed to miraculously slow time, and I could make it to work much sooner without speeding.

Music has such a prevailing influence on our life. If something special happens while we are listening to music, the event and the music become one, transcendent and timeless. It's almost as if a small world has been created, one that we can return to in a time of need. When we hear the music, it brings back those memories very clearly, much as certain smells will. The music acts as an *anchor* to those memories. It is a trigger to help us remember magic. In fact, one of the songs that I listened to when I first opened my office was 'Xanadu' by Olivia Newton-John, and the lyrics were about believing in magic.

I listened to my exercise song while using an elliptical machine so that the music and the exercise would be anchored together into my body and mind. (I used an elliptical machine because we have winter where I live, and an elliptical machine is much better than fighting ice and snowdrifts.) Since most songs last only four minutes, I played the song, and then I played it again. I played it eight times while exercising to reach 30 minutes of playing time.

So, it only has to be one song, but this song should be significant to you. The key is that it has to be a song that you don't hear all the time on the radio. It has to be something special, something that you really, really like; something that is *inspirational, has a good beat*, and *energizes you.* And it has to be one song. I have tried it with several songs and with a whole CD, but it doesn't work the same. It has to be a repetitive song, one that makes you want to move, one that makes you want to get up and dance, and ideally one that has some kind of spiritual or inspirational meaning to you and can put you in a dream state and leave you in a good space.

You need to find out how long the song is, and how many times you have to play it to reach 30 minutes.

Next, you have to exercise six to ten times while listening to the song, so that song and exercise are anchored in your brain. This may sound difficult, particularly if you haven't done any exercise in years, but think about it: if you only have to exercise eight to ten times before you can just play the music and your body *thinks* you are exercising, it isn't so bad, is it?

Exercising ten times while listening to the music is better, but six is good. This means you should exercise three to four times the first week and three to four times the next week while listening to the song.

At first, you should do aerobic exercise. It can be either running or walking or another form of aerobic exercise, but it has to be aerobic exercise because it is a proven fact that this is the best form of exercise to help release weight. In fact, if you did aerobic exercise four times a week for only 30 minutes a day, you would actually find your perfect weight sooner rather than later.

I know that when some people are starting out they can't do 30 minutes on an exercise (elliptical) machine, let alone run for 30 minutes, so it is best to start slowly. When you have gone as far as you can the first day, then the next day go a little farther.

You may only do 10 minutes of exercise the first day, 20 the second day, and 30 on the third day. But you only need to do 30 minutes of exercise at least six to eight times to anchor the music.

I know some people will be resistant to this idea. The first thing some might think to themselves is, *Ooh, I don't want to exercise ten times, or even six times.* This is the way that their subconscious is keeping them safe. Belief work before the start of the exercise may eliminate this kind of resistance.

An exercise plan that fits your lifestyle is also incredibly important. Even ten minutes a day can make a difference. One suggestion might be to use weight training as a supplement to the aerobic exercise as you are listening to your special music. Weight resistance has the following benefits: it builds muscles and lowers glucose, even when you are at rest. It helps the body to use insulin correctly and prevents injuries by building strong muscles and bones. Alternating between upper body and lower body is a good regimen. To begin with, use very light weights. Start with five to eight repetitions, gradually working up to 15 to 20 repetitions.

Once you have anchored exercise to the music, you will have to exercise periodically to keep it anchored – maybe once a week or once every two weeks. But when you hear your special song again, you will soon be back exercising because you will feel like it again – and you might not have to do it for as long as you think.

A long time ago a study was carried out regarding exercise. The researchers found that in just 8 minutes of exercise you go through the whole routine of your heart working as it would in 30 minutes. I believe this to be true. I have found that in 8 minutes, your body goes through all the same physical reactions that it does in 30 minutes of exercise. In fact, you could actually exercise for only 8 minutes a day and almost get the same effect as if you exercised for 30 minutes. So, eventually, you may only have to listen to the music for eight minutes to stimulate your mind to stimulate your body into thinking it is exercising, *and to want to exercise again.* You will need to really exercise for at least eight minutes a day every couple of weeks to re-anchor this thought-form into your body, but the trick is that it does make you want to exercise again!

EXERCISE WITHOUT EXERCISE

When I started to use this technique on myself, I dropped two to three pounds (around a kilogram) every other day. Because I was dropping weight so quickly, I got a total blood panel done to make sure I had nothing wrong with my thyroid. It was fine, and my cholesterol was beautiful. My doctor was encouraged and wanted to know what I was doing. When I told him I was exercising, he said, 'Continue the exercise program that you are on.'

So, here it is, in full…

My Secret Exercise

Either guide a client or yourself through the process in the following way:

- Center yourself in your heart and visualize going down into Mother Earth, which is a part of All That Is.
- Visualize bringing up energy through your feet, opening each chakra to the crown chakra. In a beautiful ball of light, go out to the universe.
- Go beyond the universe, past the layers of lights, past the golden light, past the jellylike substance that is the Laws, into a pearly iridescent snow-white light, into the Seventh Plane of Existence.
- Make the command: *'Creator of All That Is, I command to download myself and this music with the feeling and the knowing that whenever I listen to it, my body is exercising. Thank you. It is done. It is done. It is done.'*
- Imagine the energy coming down into your space through every cell of your body.
- When you have finished, connect back to the energy of All That Is, take a deep breath in, and make an energy break if you so choose.
- Find some music you love and exercise to it six to ten times. You can do whatever exercise you want, as

long as it is aerobic. This will anchor that music into every cell of your body.

- Then download the feeling and knowing that every time you play the music, your body will think that it is exercising.
- Then take it a step further and download that your body was exercising every time you heard the music in the past.
- Play the song at least three times a week and, if you can, exercise to it as much as possible using aerobics or dance.

After a while, just listening to the music will make you want to exercise. And every time you listen to it, your body will think that it is exercising and you will release weight even though you are not physically exercising.

If you throw in an abdominal workout at the end when you listen to the music, your body will think you are doing an abdominal workout when you aren't actually exercising at all. This can be particularly beneficial.

I have tried this process with weights, but I found that weights don't have the same repetitive motion, and therefore the same effect. Similarly, stacking the workout with different kinds of exercise – for instance, three minutes of running and a couple of minutes of another exercise – didn't have the same effect for me. I worked on this for about six months, and I found that the real results came from aerobic exercise. Aerobic exercise makes you release weight fast and is easy to anchor, but I am

not saying that lifting weights and doing other routines won't work. Try a variety of exercise routines out and see what works for you.

You can even do your exercise while watching TV with the volume down, as long as you listen to your song while you do it. Otherwise you are just training your body to watch TV to exercise, and you may not stay consistent in your program.

You can have a different song for the different types of aerobic exercise that you choose to do. For instance, you might use a running machine one day and aerobic dance the next and use two different songs.

If you get bored with your song and want to change it, you can start the process over again. You may need to do this when you drop a layer of fat.

Whenever I hear my exercise song:

1. I want to exercise and…

2. I think I am exercising.

There are times when I don't have 30 minutes to exercise every day, but it takes me 30 minutes to get to work, so I play my song on the way there so that my body thinks it is exercising. The music is likely to be triggering the hypothalamus and the hormones in the body and reaching all the primitive parts of the brain.

I made my song very simple so I could be sure my body would go through all the motions of exercise. But I know there are parts of the song where I go through a whole series of events

in my mind. I remember a movie, I recall walking through the mountains, I see myself on my exercise machine – and all these things go through my mind when I'm driving!

THE PLATEAU OF BELIEFS AND FEARS

I had great initial success with my exercise music, but two months later I found I just didn't want to play it anymore. Listening to it brought up my beliefs, both negative and positive, about releasing weight.

Memories from a past relationship came back to me – one with a violently jealous boyfriend. In one instance, I had gone to the hospital with a bladder infection, and a nurse had begun to talk to me in a friendly manner. I knew that he was gay and only being friendly, but my boyfriend thought he was flirting with me. When we got home, he threw me across the living room in a fit of jealousy. At the time I was skinny, so now I found that I had the belief that I could get in trouble if I was skinny. I had to clear this belief and the associated feelings so that I could keep on listening to the music and continue to release the weight. This is an example of why it is so important that you continue with belief work as you release weight.

Another example arose when Guy and I went on a 40-day trip through Europe in 2011. At one point Guy left me alone for a minute in an airport. A man came over, sat down next to me, and started flirting with me. When Guy came back and glared at him, he got up, obviously disappointed, and left. This didn't upset Guy too much, but it made me really scared. With Guy by my side, I really don't have to worry about that kind of stuff. But with Guy gone and a flirtatious man sitting by me,

I had been absolutely terrified of getting into trouble with my husband. On reflection, I realized these feelings had nothing to do with my present relationship and everything to do with the relationship that was more than 20 years in the past.

Once you begin to resist the music, as I did, you'll know that another layer of beliefs needs to cleared. When you've done that, however, you'll be able to keep going and you won't be stuck at a particular weight. You'll also be fascinated by the way you gain a deeper understanding of yourself as you work on each layer of beliefs.

As I teach classes at the moment, I don't have much time to exercise, but I still listen to my exercise music every day to keep myself stimulated. As I drive home listening to the music, I can be driving, thinking of 100 things, but because I am listening to the music, I am always brought back to thinking about the elliptical machine and exercising.

If I am at home when I put on the music, I go downstairs and exercise. Honestly. I don't have to fight myself … too much.

One day my granddaughter Jena and I were in the car on the way to the store and I said to her, 'I have to exercise, Jena – you'll just have to forgive me.'

She asked, 'What are you doing, Grandma?'

I explained, 'I have to listen to this song eight times so I can get my exercise in.'

When I was six times into the song, Jena turned to me and said, 'Boy, that's working. I'm sweating like crazy!'

8

Releasing the Layers

Once you've been doing this program for about two months and are on the way to your perfect weight, you may find that you no longer want to continue with it. This is because you have hit the next layer of beliefs.

Here is what is happening: toxins in the form of emotions and physical pollutants are being released. Some of the emotions that come up will be identical to those that have already been released and replaced in belief-work sessions in the past. This is because as the fat cells in your body are added to at a certain time in your life, they hold within them the programs and feelings from that time in a kind of encapsulated, indeterminate state – of suspended animation. So, as these feelings are released through exercise, you will find that you will be dealing with the same kinds of programs as before. You may wonder why a program has 'returned.' But it hasn't 'returned' at all; it has simply been released from the fat cells where it was stored by the body to protect you.

So, as we exercise and release the layers of fat, with each layer we will have to deal with the feelings, memories, toxins, and programs laid down in that layer. And so on, as each new layer is peeled off the proverbial onion.

ONE LAYER AT A TIME...

Most of the programs you will encounter in the layers you are dropping will be fears of one kind or another:

- Fear of the jealousy of others
- Fear of being smaller
- Fear of losing yourself
- Fear of losing someone because you are different than you were
- Fear of change.

The way to deal with these fears, and any other programs and feelings in the layer you have reached, is to take a week or two off exercise and work on yourself with belief work. Then restart the exercise program. You can continue with your old song or anchor a new song that you are drawn to for the next layer of weight release.

The song that I listened to for the first layer of my weight release reminded me of how illumination, justice, and good always triumph over darkness and evil, because this was what I was experiencing and what had been encapsulated within the fat cells of that layer.

When I discovered that I was into a completely new layer, I worked on myself with belief work, and after a while I found that my needs had changed because I had replaced and released so many negative beliefs. I no longer needed the energy from the old song of duality – I needed the vigor of something new. I had listened to the old song for eight months, and it was time

to shift gears. The new song that I anchored in was about life being good and the fact that I had 'made it.' However, I found that I had to go through the full process that is explained in Step 5 to anchor the new song.

It is important to know that we don't encounter new layers of belief just because of weight release. They appear at different times in our lives, usually when we are stressed due to some kind of change. This opens new layers in the unconscious mind, and these may be beliefs that are identical to those that you think have already been released and replaced.

FEAR OF LOSING YOURSELF

If you have been heavy for a long time, releasing weight may make you feel as though you are losing yourself.

One thing that will help with this is being aware of your body. One way to do this is the following:

- Rub your body where the fat is – somewhere such as the tummy.
- As you rub the stomach area, think back in time. If you have ever been slender, go back to those memories.
- Remember how easy it was to be slender. For most people this also brings back the energy of youth.
- Then, as you continue to rub your stomach for an anchor, download these feelings from the Creator into yourself. This helps to recover the golden sunshine of youth and the feel of your perfect weight.

If the memories that are associated with the strength of youth frighten you, you need to clear those negative energies so that you are creating something new.

Being aware of your size and your body is important. I have found that people who are extremely obese rarely look at themselves in the mirror. It is only when they pass by the window glass at a department store that they become shocked by their size. Even then, there are times when they disregard what they have seen and tell themselves that they are happy the way they are.

This is a disassociation from reality and from the body. This is why you need to touch your body and see yourself as slender – it will reconnect you to your body as well as help you to move into the next layer of weight release.

FEAR OF SUCCESS

Strangely, perhaps, the issues that most often block us on the way to our perfect weight are issues of success. If you fail to move toward your perfect weight, then you tell yourself, 'OK, that didn't work. No big deal.' If you succeed, that brings forth change. Which can be scary.

One reason for this is that you will see yourself differently, and the world will see you differently, too. How will the world perceive you if you are slender and strong? With love or with jealousy? Which is it going to be? Or something else entirely? This is a fear of the unknown that you must face if you release weight.

ThetaHealing teaches that everything is a product of our belief systems – we literally create our own reality based on our

thoughts and our divinity – for we are part of God. We create our own divine reality, and it is up to us whether that reality is good, bad, or indifferent.

Therefore, we believe that not being at our perfect weight has more to do with our beliefs than we may realize. Being over- or underweight may be a projection of our self-image, and that is based on what we feel about ourselves. Again, this may be good, bad, or indifferent.

If you are overweight, there are reasons for it, and one may be that your subconscious is attempting to protect you from what it perceives as a threat. The subconscious only knows what it is taught, and if it is taught, for instance, that relationships are bad, then it will keep you heavy so that you have an excuse for not getting into a relationship.

There are many different reasons why people are heavy, as we have already seen. Each is a projection of our self-image. So as we explore our bodies and how we feel about ourselves, we see that being overweight isn't necessarily a bad self-image. Sometimes it serves its purpose in a high and divine way.

Ultimately, it is up to us to change what we believe. In ThetaHealing we want to teach people that they can have divine thoughts, divine essence, and be in the best of health. This weight program is for those people who are intuitive; who realize that there is no separation between mind, body, and soul; and who are willing to take a chance in order to get an understanding of why we do what we do and how we can change our self-projections.

9

Suggested Diets

Some people don't feel that they will release weight unless they are on a diet. This is because they have been on successful diets in the past and need the structure that a diet affords them.

THE DIABETES DIET

If you have to be on a diet, or want to be, I recommend the diabetes diet, as it teaches you to eat in small increments through the day and to count carbohydrates. But understand one thing: exercise is still the key, and in order to exercise, you have to overcome the fear that it will hurt you.

With the diabetes diet, you only eat 30 carbohydrates per meal and 15–20 carbohydrates per snack, but you have to eat three times a day and snack twice a day.

The following Diabetes Diet charts show how to count carbohydrates in different food types:

Carbohydrate Counter: Starches		
Type of Food	**Serving Size**	**Carbohydrates per Serving**
bagel	1 oz (28 g)	15
reduced-calorie bread	2 slices (1½ oz/ 45 g)	15
white/whole wheat/rye bread	1 slice (1 oz/28 g)	15
crisp breadsticks (4 x ½ in/1 cm)	4 (⅔ oz/18 g)	15
English muffin	½	15
hot dog/hamburger bun	½ (1 oz/28 g)	15
naan bread (8 x 2 in/5 cm)	¼	15
pancake (4 in/10 cm across)	1	15
pita bread (6 in/15 cm across)	1	15
small plain roll	1 (1 oz/28 g)	15
unfrosted raisin bread	1 slice (1 oz/28 g)	15
corn tortilla (6 in/15 cm across)	1	15
flour tortilla (6 in/15 cm across)	1	15
flour tortilla (10 in/25 cm across)	⅓	15
reduced-fat waffle (4 in/10 cm square/across)	1	15
bran cereals	½ cup (75 g)	15
Bulgur wheat	½ cup (75 g)	15
cooked cereals	½ cup (75 g)	15
unsweetened cereals	¾ cup (113 g)	15
dry cornmeal	3 tbsp	15
cous cous	⅓ cup (50 g)	15
dry flour	3 tbsp	15
low-fat granola	¼ cup (38 g)	15
grape nuts	¼ cup (38 g)	15
grits	½ cup (75 g)	15

Type of Food	Serving Size	Carbohydrates per Serving
kasha	½ cup (75 g)	15
millet	⅓ cup (50 g)	15
muesli	¼ cup (38 g)	15
oats	½ cup (75 g)	15
pasta	⅓ cup (50 g)	15
puffed cereal	1½ cups (225 g)	15
white/brown rice	⅓ cup (50 g)	15
Shredded Wheat	½ cup (75 g)	15
sugar-frosted cereal	½ cup (75 g)	15
wheat germ	3 tbsp	15
baked beans	⅓ cup (50 g)	15
corn (sweet corn)	½ cup (100 g)	15
large corn cob (corn on the cob)	½ cob (150 g)	15
mixed vegetables	1 cup (200 g)	15
peas	½ cup (/100 g)	15
plantains	½ cup (100 g)	15
boiled potato	½ medium (75 g)	15
baked potato w/skin	¼ large (75 g)	15
mashed potatoes	½ cup (100 g)	15
winter squash (acorn, butternut, pumpkin)	1 cup (200 g)	15
yam, sweet potato, plain	½ cup (100 g)	15
animal crackers	8	15
Graham cracker/Digestive biscuit (2½ in/6 cm diameter)	3	15
matzoh	¾ oz (20 g)	15
Melba toast	4 slices	15
oyster crackers	20	15
popcorn (popped, no fat added, low-fat microwave)	3 cups (575 g)	15
pretzels	¾ oz (20 g)	15

Carbohydrate Counter: Starches (cont.)		
Type of Food	**Serving Size**	**Carbohydrates per Serving**
rice cakes (4 in/10 cm across)	2	15
saltine-type crackers	6	15
potato chips (crisps) (fat-free, baked)	15–20 (¾ oz/20 g)	15
whole-wheat crackers (no fat added)	2–5 (¾ oz/20 g)	15
beans and peas (garbanzo, pinto, kidney, white, split, black-eyed)	½ cup (100 g)	15
Lima beans	⅔ cup (125 g)	15
lentils	½ cup (75 g)	15
miso	3 tbsp	15
biscuit (2½ in/6 cm across)	1	15
corn bread (2 in/5 cm cube)	1 (2 oz/60 g)	15
chow mein noodles	½ cup (100 g)	15
round butter-type crackers	6	15
croutons	1 cup (200 g)	15
French fries (oven baked)	1 cup (50 g)	15
hummus	⅓ cup (65 g)	15
muffin (5 oz/150 g)	⅕ (1 oz/28 g)	15
sandwich crackers (cheese/ peanut butter filling)	3	15
snack chips (potato [crisps], tortilla)	9–13 (¾ oz/20 g)	15
prepared bread stuffing	⅓ cup (65 g)	15
5 in/12 cm taco shell	2	15
whole-wheat crackers	4–7 (1 oz/28 g)	15

Carbohydrate Counter: Fruit		
Type of Food	**Serving Size**	**Carbohydrates per Serving**
small, unpeeled apple	1 (4 oz/120 g)	15
unsweetened applesauce	½ cup (100 g)	15
dried apples	4 rings	15
fresh apricots	4 whole (5½ oz/165 g)	15
dried apricots	8 halves	15
canned apricots	½ cup (100 g)	15
small banana	1 (4 oz/120 g)	15
blackberries	¾ cup (150 g)	15
blueberries (bilberries)	¾ cup (150 g)	15
small cantaloupe melon	⅓ (11 oz/325 g)	15
sweet fresh cherries	12 (3 oz/75 g)	15
sweet canned cherries	½ cup (100 g)	15
dates	3	15
fresh figs	1½ large (3½ oz/100 g)	15
dried figs	1½	15
canned fruit cocktail	½ cup (100 g)	15
large fresh grapefruit	½ (11 oz/325 g)	15
canned grapefruit sections	¾ cup (150 g)	15
small grapes	17 (3 oz/75 g)	15
honeydew melon	1 slice (10 oz /300 g)	15
kiwi fruit	1 (3½ oz/100 g)	15
canned mandarin oranges	¾ cup (150 g)	15
small mango	½ (5½ oz /165 g)	15
small nectarine	1 (5 oz/150 g)	15
small orange	1 (6½ oz/190 g)	15
papaya	½ (8 oz/250 g)	15
fresh medium peach	1 (6 oz/175 g)	15
canned peaches	1 (6 oz/175 g)	15
large fresh pear	½ (4 oz/125 g)	15

Carbohydrate Counter: Fruit (cont.)		
Type of Food	**Serving Size**	**Carbohydrates per Serving**
canned pears	½ cup (100 g)	15
fresh pineapple	¾ cup (150 g)	15
canned pineapple	½ cup (100 g)	15
small fresh plums	2 (5 oz/150 g)	15
canned plums	½ cup (100 g)	15
dried plums (prunes)	3	15
raisins	2 tbsp	15
raspberries	1 cup (200 g)	15
strawberries (whole)	1¼ cup (250 g)	15
small tangerines	2 (8 oz/250 g)	15
watermelon	1 slice (13½ oz/415 g)	15
unsweetened apple juice	4 fl oz (120 ml)	15
cranberry juice cocktail	3 fl oz (80 ml)	15
reduced-calorie cranberry juice cocktail	8 fl oz (240 ml)	15
100% fruit juice blends	3 fl oz (80 ml)	15
grape juice	3 fl oz (80 ml)	15
grapefruit juice	4 fl oz (120 ml)	15
orange juice	4 fl oz (120 ml)	15
pineapple juice	4 fl oz (120 ml)	15
prune juice	3 fl oz (80 ml)	15

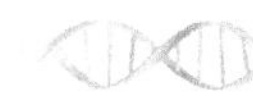

Carbohydrate Counter: Dairy		
Type of Food	**Serving Size**	**Carbohydrates per Serving**
fat-free milk	8 fl oz (240 ml)	12
0.5% milk	8 fl oz (240 ml)	12
1% milk	8 fl oz (240 ml)	12
2% milk	8 fl oz (240 ml)	12
sweet acidophilus milk	8 fl oz (240 ml)	12
whole milk	8 fl oz (240 ml)	12
evaporated whole milk	4 fl oz (120 ml)	12
goat's milk	8 fl oz (240 ml)	12
buttermilk (low-fat/fat-free)	8 fl oz (240 ml)	12
evaporated, fat-free milk	4 fl oz (120 ml)	12
fat-free, dry milk	⅓ cup (47 g)	12
soy (soya) milk (low-fat/ fat-free)	8 fl oz (240 ml)	12
yogurt (fat-free, flavored, sweetened with fructose)	6 oz (175 g)	12
plain, fat-free yogurt	6 oz (175 g)	12
kefir	8 fl oz (240 ml)	12
plain yogurt (made from whole milk)	8 oz (250 g)	12

Carbohydrate Counter: Combination Foods		
Type of Food	**Serving Size**	**Carbohydrates per Serving**
tuna noodle casserole	1 cup (250 g)	30
lasagna	1 cup (250 g)	30
spaghetti with meatballs	1 cup (250 g)	30
chili with beans	1 cup (250 g)	30
macaroni cheese	1 cup (250 g)	30
stir-fry vegetables (without noodles or rice)	2 cups (500 g)	15
tuna/chicken salad	½ cup (100 g)	8
frozen dinners	approx. 14–17 oz (425–525 g)	45
meatless, soy-based burger	3 oz (75 g)	8
vegetable/starched-based burger	3 oz (75 g)	15
thin-crust cheese pizza	4½–5 oz (140–150 g)	30
thin-crust meat-topping pizza	5 oz (150 g)	30
pot pie (pie)	1 (7 oz/200 g)	38
entrée/meal with fewer than 340 calories	8–11 oz (250–325 g)	30–45
bean soup	8 fl oz (240 ml)	15
cream soup	8 fl oz (240 ml)	15
instant soup	6 fl oz (175 ml) prepared	15
instant soup with beans/ lentils	8 fl oz (240 ml) prepared	38
tomato soup	8 fl oz (240 ml)	15
split-pea soup	4 fl oz (120 ml)	15
vegetable, beef, chicken noodle, basic broth-type soups	8 fl oz (240 ml)	15

Cabohydrate Counter: Snacks		
Type of Food	**Serving Size**	**Carbohydrates per Serving**
unfrosted angel food cake	2 oz (60 g)	30
small, unfrosted brownie	1 oz (28 g)	15
unfrosted cake	1 oz (28 g)	15
frosted cake	1 oz (28 g)	30
cookie/cookie sandwich with cream filling (biscuits)	2 small (⅔ oz/18 g)	15
jellied cranberry sauce	¼ cup (50 g)	23
frosted cupcake	1 small (about 2 oz/60 g)	30
sugar-free cookie (biscuit)	3 small/1 large (¾–1 oz/21–28 g)	15
plain cake doughnut	1 medium (1½ oz/40 g)	23
glazed doughnuts	1 x 3¾ in/8.5 cm across (2 oz/60 g)	30
energy/sport/breakfast bar	1 bar (2 oz/60 g)	30
fruit cobbler	½ cup (100 g)	45
100% fruit juice bars, frozen	1 bar (3 oz/90 g)	15
chewy fruit snacks	1 roll (¾ oz/21 g)	15
100% fruit spreads	1½ tbsp	15
regular gelatin	½ cup (50 g)	15
ginger snaps	3	15
regular/low-fat granola/ snack bar	1 bar (1 oz/28 g)	23
honey	1 tbsp	15
regular ice-cream	½ cup (100 g)	15
light ice-cream	½ cup (100 g)	15
low-fat ice-cream	½ cup (100 g)	23
fat-free sugarless ice-cream	½ cup (100 g)	15
regular jam/jelly	1 tbsp	15
whole chocolate milk	1 cup (240 ml)	30

Cabohydrate Counter: Snacks (cont.)		
Type of Food	**Serving Size**	**Carbohydrates per Serving**
fruit pie (2 crusts)	⅙ of 8 in/20 cm prepared pie	45
pumpkin/custard pie	⅛ of 8 in/20 cm prepared pie	30
regular pudding (made with reduced-fat milk)	½ cup (100 g)	30
sugar/fat-free pudding	½ cup (100 g)	15
reduced-calorie meal replacement shake	4 fl oz (120 ml)	23
plain low-fat/fat-free rice milk	8 fl oz (240 ml)	15
flavored low-fat rice milk	8 fl oz (240 ml)	23
fat-free salad dressing	2 fl oz (60 ml)	15
sherbet, sorbet	½ cup (100 g)	30
canned pasta sauce	½ cup (100 g)	15
sports drink	8 fl oz (240 ml)	15
sugar	1 tbsp	15
Danish pastry/sweet roll	1 (2½ oz/65 g)	38
light syrup	2 tbsp	15
regular syrup	1 tbsp	15
regular syrup	4 tbsp	60
vanilla wafers	5	15
frozen yogurt	½ cup (100 g)	15
fat-free frozen yogurt	⅓ cup (65 g)	15
low-fat yogurt with fruit	1 cup (200 g)	45

Carbohydrate Counter: Fast Food		
Type of Food	**Serving Size**	**Carbohydrates per Serving**
burrito	1 (5–7 oz/150–200 g)	45
chicken nuggets	6	15
chicken breast and wing (breaded and fried)	1 of each	15
grilled chicken sandwich	1	30
hot chicken wings	6 (5 oz/150 g)	0
fish sandwich with tartar sauce	1	45
French fries (chips)	1 medium serving (5 oz/150 g)	60
regular hamburger	1	30
large hamburger	1	30
hot dog with bun	1	15
individual pan pizza	1	75
thin-crust cheese pizza	6 oz (175 g)	38
thin-crust meat pizza	6 oz (175 g)	38
soft-serve cone	1 small (5 oz/150 g)	38
regular submarine sandwich	1 x 6 in (15 cm)	53
sub sandwich with fewer than 6 grams of fat	1 x 6 in (15 cm)	45
hard/soft-shell taco	1 (3–3½ oz/85–100 g)	15

Carbohydrate Counter: 'Free' Food You can eat three servings of these at one time (all the same or all different).		
Type of Food	**Serving Size**	**Carbohydrates per Serving**
cream cheese (fat-free)	1 tbsp	5
creamers, non-dairy, liquid	1 tbsp	5
creamers, non-dairy, powdered	2 tbsp	5
mayonnaise, fat-free	1 tbsp	5
mayonnaise, reduced fat	1 tsp	5
margarine, fat-free	4 tbsp	5
margarine, reduced fat	1 tsp	5
Miracle Whip, fat-free	1 tbsp	5
Miracle Whip, reduced fat	1 tsp	5
salad dressing, fat-free or low fat	1 tbsp	5
salad dressing, fat-free, Italian	2 tbsp	5
sour cream, fat-free, reduced fat	1 tbsp	5
whipped topping regular	1 tbsp	5
whipped topping, light or fat-free	2 tbsp	5

Carbohydrate Counter: Sugar-Free Foods		
Type of Food	**Serving Size**	**Carbohydrates per Serving**
candy, hard	1	5
gelatin dessert, gelatin, unflavored gum, jam or jelly, light	2 tsp	5
syrup	2 tbsp	5

Carbohydrate Counter: Drinks		
Type of Food	**Serving Size**	**Carbohydrates per Serving**
cocoa powder, unsweetened	1 tbsp	5
coffee, black	any	0
diet soft drinks	any	0
sugar-free drink mixes	any	0
tea, black or herbal	any	0
tonic water, sugar free	any	0

Carbohydrate Counter: Condiments		
Type of Food	**Serving Size**	**Carbohydrates per Serving**
catsup (ketchup)	1 tbsp	5
horseradish	1 tbsp	5
lemon juice	1 tbsp	5
lime juice	1 tbsp	5
mustard	1 tbsp	5
pickle relish	1 tbsp	5
pickles, dill	1½ medium	5
pickles, sweet (bread and butter/cucumber)	2 slices	5
pickles, sweet (gherkin)	¾ oz (20 g)	5
salsa	¼ cup (50 g)	5
soy sauce, regular or light	1 tbsp	5
taco sauce	1 tbsp	5
vinegar	1 tbsp	0
yogurt	2 tbsp	5

Carbohydrate Counter: Seasonings		
Type of Food	**Serving Size**	**Carbohydrates per Serving**
flavoring extracts	any	0
garlic	any	0
herbs, fresh or dried	any	0
pimento	any	0
spices	any	0
tabasco or hot pepper sauce	any	0
wine, used in cooking	any	0
Worcestershire sauce	any	0

Carbohydrate Counter: Vegetables one vegetable exchange (½ cup [100 g] cooked or 1 cup [200 g] raw) equals 5 carbohydrates		
Type of Food	**Serving Size**	**Carbohydrates per Serving**
artichokes	½ cup (100 g) cooked or 1 cup (200 g) raw	5
artichoke hearts	½ cup (100 g) cooked or 1 cup (200 g) raw	5
asparagus	½ cup (100 g) cooked or 1 cup (200 g) raw	5
beans (green, wax, Italian)	½ cup (100 g) cooked or 1 cup (200 g) raw	5
bean sprouts	½ cup (100 g) cooked or 1 cup (200 g) raw	5
beets (beetroot)	½ cup (100 g) cooked or 1 cup (200 g) raw	5
broccoli	½ cup (100 g) cooked or 1 cup (200 g) raw	5
Brussels sprouts	½ cup (100 g) cooked or 1 cup (200 g) raw	5
cabbage	½ cup (100 g) cooked or 1 cup (200 g) raw	5

Cabohydrate Counter: Vegetables (cont.)		
Type of Food	**Serving Size**	**Carbohydrates per Serving**
carrots	½ cup (100 g) cooked or 1 cup (200 g) raw	5
cauliflower	½ cup (100 g) cooked or 1 cup (200 g) raw	5
celery	½ cup (100 g) cooked or 1 cup (200 g) raw	5
cucumber	½ cup (100 g) cooked or 1 cup (200 g) raw	5
eggplant (aubergine)	½ cup (100 g) cooked or 1 cup (200 g) raw	5
green onions or scallions (spring onions)	½ cup (100 g) cooked or 1 cup (200 g) raw	5
greens (collard, kale, mustard, turnips)	½ cup (100 g) cooked or 1 cup (200 g) raw	5
kohlrabi	½ cup (100 g) cooked or 1 cup (200 g) raw	5
leeks	½ cup (100 g) cooked or 1 cup (200 g) raw	5
mixed vegetables (without corn, peas, or pasta)	½ cup (100 g) cooked or 1 cup (200 g) raw	5
mushrooms	½ cup (100 g) cooked or 1 cup (200 g) raw	5
okra	½ cup (100 g) cooked or 1 cup (200 g) raw	5
onions	½ cup (100 g) cooked or 1 cup (200 g) raw	5
pea pods (mangetout)	½ cup (100 g) cooked or 1 cup (200 g) raw	5
peppers (all varieties)	½ cup (100 g) cooked or 1 cup (200 g) raw	5
radishes	½ cup (100 g) cooked or 1 cup (200 g) raw	5
salad greens (endive, escarole, lettuce, romaine, spinach)	½ cup (100 g) cooked or 1 cup (200 g) raw	5

Cabohydrate Counter: Vegetables (cont.)		
Type of Food	**Serving Size**	**Carbohydrates per Serving**
sauerkraut	½ cup (100 g) cooked or 1 cup (200 g) raw	5
spinach	½ cup (100 g) cooked or 1 cup (200 g) raw	5
summer squash	½ cup (100 g) cooked or 1 cup (200 g) raw	5
tomatoes	½ cup (100 g) cooked or 1 cup (200 g) raw	5
tomatoes, canned	½ cup (100 g) cooked or 1 cup (200 g) raw	5
tomato sauce	½ cup (100 g) cooked or 1 cup (200 g) raw	5
tomato/vegetable juice	4 fl oz/120 ml cooked or 8 fl oz/240 ml raw	5
turnips	½ cup (100 g) cooked or 1 cup (200 g) raw	5
water chestnuts	½ cup (100 g) cooked or 1 cup (200 g) raw	5
watercress	½ cup (100 g) cooked or 1 cup (200 g) raw	5
zucchini (courgette)	½ cup (100 g) cooked or 1 cup (200 g) raw	5

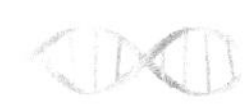

THE SACRED HEART MEMORIAL HOSPITAL DIET

This diet is for those who want to release weight quickly. It is from the Sacred Heart Memorial Hospital and is used with heart patients who need to lose weight rapidly, usually before surgery.

Basic Fat-Burning Soup

This soup can be eaten whenever you are hungry and you can eat as much of it as you want. It will not add many calories to your diet, and the more of it you eat, the more weight you will lose. Fill a Thermos with it in the morning if you will be away from home during the day.

Note: If you were to eat the soup alone, for indefinite periods, you would suffer malnutrition.

Ingredients

12 green onions/scallions (spring onions), chopped
1 or 2 cans of chopped tomatoes
1 large head of cabbage, chopped
2 green peppers
1 bunch celery
1 packet of Lipton (or other) onion soup mix
Optional: Cilantro (coriander) or parsley, chopped
Seasonings: Salt, pepper, curry powder, bouillon, or hot sauce (Tabasco)

Method

Cut the vegetables into small to medium pieces, add the onion soup mix, canned tomatoes, and seasonings and cover with pure filtered water. Boil for 5–10 minutes and then simmer until vegetables are soft.

The Program

Day One

Eat only the soup and fruit – all kinds of fruit, except bananas. Cantaloupe and watermelon are lower in calories.

For drinks: Unsweetened tea, cranberry juice, or purified water.

Day Two

Don't eat any fruit. Do eat vegetables. Eat until you are stuffed with all the fresh, raw, or canned vegetables you like, though do try to eat green leafy vegetables and stay away from beans, corn, and peas.

Have as much of the soup as you want.

At dinnertime, reward yourself with a plain baked potato.

Day Three

Eat all the soup, fruit, and vegetables that you want. Don't have a baked potato.

Day Four

If you have eaten for three days as above and haven't cheated, you will find on the morning of the fourth day that you have lost 5–7 pounds (7–9 kg). I personally lost 9 pounds (11 kg).

On the fourth day, eat as many as three bananas with skimmed milk and drink as many glasses of purified water as you can. (I added fresh lemon juice to my purified water.) Bananas are high in calories and carbohydrates, and so is the milk.

However, today your body will need the potassium and the carbs, proteins, and calories to lessen your cravings for sweets.

Eat the soup at least twice today.

Day Five

Beef and tomatoes. You may have 10–20 oz (300–600 g) of beef and a can of tomatoes or as many as six fresh tomatoes today. Try to drink at least six to eight glasses of purified water to wash away the uric acid in your body. Eat the soup at least once today. (I ate broiled salmon in place of red meat.)

Day Six

Beef and veggies. Eat beef and vegetables to your heart's content today. You can have two or three steaks if you like. Eat green leafy vegetables. No baked potato. Be sure to eat the soup at least once.

Day Seven

Brown rice, unsweetened fruit juice, and vegetables. Stuff yourself. Be sure to have the soup at least once today.

By the end of the seventh day, or the morning of the eighth day, if you have not cheated you will have lost 10–17 pounds (4.5–7.5 kg) If you have lost more than 15 pounds (6.5 kg), stay off the diet for two days before resuming the diet again at Day One.

Continue it for as long as you wish, and feel the difference. After only seven days, as well as feeling lighter by at least 10 pounds (4.5 kg), you will have an abundance of energy.

This seven-day eating plan can be used as often as you like. It is fast and fat burning, and the secret is that you will burn more calories than you take in. As a matter of fact, if correctly followed, it will clean your system of impurities and give you a feeling of well-being as never before.

Because everyone's digestive system is different, this diet will affect everyone differently. In general, however, after Day Three you will have more energy than when you began. After being on the diet for several days, you will find that your bowel movements have changed. Eat a cup of bran or fiber. Although you can have black coffee with this diet, you may find that you don't need the caffeine after the third day. (I chose not to consume coffee.)

The diet does not lend itself to drinking any alcoholic beverages at any time because of the removal of fat buildup in your system. Go off the diet at least 24 hours before any intake of alcohol.

Other definite no-nos are fried foods, chicken skin, bread, and carbonated drinks (including diet). Stick with purified water, unsweetened tea, white coffee, unsweetened fruit juice, cranberry juice, and skimmed milk. You can eat broiled or baked chicken or broiled fish instead of meat only on one of the beef days, but you need the high protein in the beef on the other days.

The basic fat-burning soup can be eaten anytime you feel hungry – the more of it you eat, the more weight you will release. Eat as much as you wish.

Prescribed medication will not hurt you on this diet.

Continue this plan for as long as you wish, and feel the difference both mentally and physically.

Resources

THETAHEALING® CLASSES

ThetaHealing is an energy-healing modality founded by Vianna Stibal, based in Ammon, Idaho, with certified instructors around the world. The classes and books of ThetaHealing are designed as therapeutic self-help guides to develop the ability of the mind to heal. ThetaHealing includes the following books, manuals, and classes:

Classes taught by Vianna and certified ThetaHealing instructors:

Vianna's DNA 2 Course

Vianna's DNA 2 Advanced Course: The Planes of Existence

Vianna's Intuitive Anatomy Course

Vianna's Children of the Rainbow Course

ThetaHealing Manifesting and Abundance Course

ThetaHealing Diseases and Disorder Class

ThetaHealing World Relations Class

Certification classes taught exclusively by Vianna at the ThetaHealing Institute of Knowledge:

Vianna's Children of the Rainbow Teachers Course

Vianna's DNA 2 Teachers Course

Vianna's DNA 2 Advanced Teachers Course

Vianna's Intuitive Anatomy Teachers Course

ThetaHealing Diseases and Disorder Certification Class

ThetaHealing World Relations Certification Class

DNA 3

BOOKS

Titles currently available:

ThetaHealing® (Hay House, 2010)

Advanced ThetaHealing® (Hay House, 2011)

ThetaHealing® Diseases and Disorders (Hay House, 2011)

On the Wings of Prayer (Hay House, 2012)

Class Manuals

ThetaHealing™ Practitioner Manual

Vianna's Teacher's Manual

Vianna's DNA 2 Advanced Manual

Vianna's DNA 2 Advanced Teacher's Manual

Vianna's Intuitive Anatomy Manual

Vianna's Intuitive Anatomy Teacher's Manual

Vianna's Rainbow Children's Young Children's Manual

Vianna's Rainbow Children's Young Adult's Manual

Vianna's Rainbow Children's Teacher's Manual

ThetaHealing Manifesting and Abundance Manual

For further information about schedules for ThetaHealing classes, call (208) 524-0808 at the ThetaHealing Institute of Knowledge, Ammon, Idaho 83406, USA; e-mail: vianna@thetahealing.com; website: www.thetahealing.com

Index

This index is arranged in word-by-word alphabetical order.

G

H

I

J,K

L

M

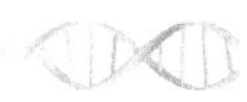

NOTES

Notes

Join the **HAY HOUSE** *Family*

As the leading self-help, mind, body and spirit publisher in the UK, we'd like to welcome you to our community so that you can keep updated with the latest news, including new releases, exclusive offers, author events and more.

Sign up at www.hayhouse.co.uk/register

Like us on Facebook at Hay House UK

Follow us on Twitter @HayHouseUK

www.hayhouse.co.uk

Hay House Publishers
Astley House, 33 Notting Hill Gate, London W11 3JQ
020 3675 2450 info@hayhouse.co.uk

ABOUT THE AUTHOR

Vianna Stibal is a young grandmother, an artist, and a writer. Her natural charisma and compassion for those in need of help have also led to her being known as a healer, intuitive, and teacher.

After being taught how to connect with the Creator to co-create and facilitate the unique process called ThetaHealing®, Vianna knew that she must share this gift with as many people as she could. It was this love and appreciation for the Creator and humanity that allowed her to develop the ability to see clearly into the human body and witness many instant healings.

Her encyclopedic knowledge of the body's systems and deep understanding of the human psyche, based on her own experience, as well as the insight given to her by the Creator, make Vianna the perfect practitioner of this amazing technique. She has successfully worked with such medical challenges as hepatitis C, Epstein-Barr virus, AIDS, herpes, various types of cancer; and many other disorders, diseases, and genetic defects.

Vianna knows that the ThetaHealing technique is teachable, but beyond that she knows that it needs to be taught. She conducts seminars all over the world to teach people of all races, beliefs, and religions. She has trained teachers and practitioners who are working in 25 countries, but her work will not stop there! She is committed to spreading this healing paradigm throughout the world.

www.thetahealing.com

Lightning Source UK Ltd.
Milton Keynes UK
UKOW06f0039010416

271297UK00001B/24/P